Crepe Cookbook For Total Beginners

Josephu .X Jamesu

Introduction

This book is a comprehensive guide that explores the art of making crepes and provides a wide range of delicious recipes for both sweet and savory crepes. Whether you're a novice in the kitchen or an experienced cook, this book offers step-by-step instructions and creative ideas to help you master the art of crepe making.

The book begins with an introduction to the art of crepe making, providing insights into the history and versatility of crepes. It explains the basics of preparing the crepe batter and shares tips and techniques for achieving the perfect consistency and texture.

The following sections focus on different types of crepe batters, including traditional sweet crepes, savory buckwheat galettes, gluten-free crepes, vegan crepes, keto-friendly crepes, and paleo-friendly crepes. Each section includes a variety of recipes tailored to specific dietary preferences, allowing you to explore different flavors and ingredients.

The book then dives into the world of savory crepes, offering an array of recipes that feature delicious fillings and combinations. From Red Beet Crepes with Spring Peas and Goat Cheese to Spicy Lamb and Chickpea Crepes, you'll find savory options to satisfy your taste buds.

For those with a sweet tooth, the book provides a wide selection of sweet crepe recipes. Lemon and Sugar Crepes, Crepes Suzette, Peach Cobbler Crepes, and Chocolate Cheesecake Crepes are just a few examples of the delightful creations you can make.

Additionally, the book goes beyond just crepes and explores other creative uses for crepe batter. You'll find recipes for a Rainbow Crepe Cake, Crepe Crisps, Crepe and Fruit Brochettes, Frozen Peanut Butter Cup Crepes, and more.

Each recipe is accompanied by clear instructions, ingredient lists, and beautiful photographs that inspire and guide you through the cooking process. Whether you're looking to impress your family and friends with a gourmet crepe meal or simply want to enjoy a tasty treat, This book is an excellent resource for all crepe enthusiasts.

Contents

Chapter 1

THE ART OF CREPE MAKING

This chapter will familiarize you with the history of crepes, how they have evolved over the years, and what you need to make delicious crepes at home. Young and old, rich and poor, crepes are enjoyed by just about everyone!

What Are Crepes?

A crepe is made by pouring a very thin batter onto a hot surface. The batter is then flipped, filled with just about anything you can imagine, folded, and served in minutes. There is a crepe for almost every eating occasion: breakfast, lunch, dinner, dessert, or quick snack. The crepe itself is made with simple ingredients—traditionally, eggs, milk, some type of flour, and salt—but can be varied to suit most palates and dietary restrictions.

A History of Crepes

Although many countries have their own version of crepes, the first crepes were thought to originate in the northwest part of France called Bretagne, which we now know as Brittany.

The landscape was rugged and rocky with steep, wild cliffs. The climate was not conducive for growing much of anything until the 12th century, when traders introduced a new crop—buckwheat—to the region, where it thrived. This grain provided significant protein and fiber to the local diet, improving the health of the people and becoming a staple ingredient in traditional Breton dishes.

A favorite way to eat buckwheat was to grind it into flour and combine it with other ingredients people had on hand, such as eggs and milk. Once mixed, it was poured onto a heated cast-iron plate and cooked until the edges curled. This is the derivation of the name "crepe," from the Latin word *crispa*, meaning "curl." It was then filled with other local ingredients, such as eggs, ham, cheese, or fruit. These buckwheat crepes were known as "galettes." It was not until the 20th century that white flour became a staple ingredient for crepes, as it was prohibitively expensive until that time.

Crepes have also played a role in some religious occasions. In France, the second of February is La Chandeleur, or Crepe Day, and is celebrated in anticipation of Lent. During Lent, meat and its byproducts, including eggs, milk, and animal fats, were prohibited. Since there was no refrigeration, people tried to eat up these perishables before Ash Wednesday, mixing these ingredients with flour to make crepes. Many customs have grown up around this Lenten holiday, such as tossing a crepe into the air with one hand and catching it in the pan while holding a piece of money in the other. This assured the flipper a year without financial worry.

My favorite legend about the history of crepes is the invention of the dessert Crepes Suzette. According to the story, which may or may not be true, a young assistant waiter created the dish entirely by mistake in 1895 at a café in Paris. While preparing dessert for the Prince of Wales, the waiter accidentally set the dish of crepes soaked in cordial on fire. He feared the dessert was ruined, but after tasting it, found that the flame was the perfect way to bring together the delicious harmony of flavors. The prince adored the dish and named it after his lovely dinner guest, a beautiful French girl named Suzette.

Crepes Today

Crepes have come a long way since the galettes of Brittany in the 12th century. They have become increasingly popular in every culture because they are quick and simple to make at home and do not require expensive specialty pans. A variety of affordable crepe makers are available to make cooking them even easier, which we will discuss later in this chapter.

With today's wide variety of dietary preferences and needs, crepes have become remarkably versatile in their ingredients. Batter can be made gluten-free, keto-friendly, paleo-friendly, vegan, or served the classic French way. No matter what batter you choose, crepes are still cooked in the traditonal way, by pouring a thin layer of batter on a heated surface, flipping it, and then filling and folding.

Making Crepes Like a Champ

Although simple and quick, there is an art to making a great crepe. The most delicious crepes have a crispy golden texture on the outside and are heated to perfection, to melt or warm the combination of ingredients enclosed within.

The temperature of the pan is crucial. Wait until the butter or oil has the perfect color and bubbliness, then rush to pour the batter and spread it thinly and evenly. Next is the flip, which is often the most intimidating part for novices. But with proper instruction, flipping is a piece of crepe!

REGULAR PANS

You don't need a fancy pan to make your crepes. Most pans will work as long as they have a heavy, flat bottom. But as with any task, getting the right equipment makes it much easier to produce the perfect crepe.

Using a standard sauté pan is fine, but your crepes do risk being uneven, and they may stick and be more difficult to turn if you haven't used enough butter or oil. You can also use a skillet or frying pan with slanted or curved sides, as long as the base of the pan is the size of the crepe you want to cook.

The traditional pans for cooking crepes are cast iron. Though they take longer to heat up, they distribute heat very evenly. Steel pans also work well. They usually have a flat base and sloping sides.

There is some debate over using regular or nonstick pans. While seasoning a cast-iron or steel pan makes it nonstick, another option is to use a more modern pan with a resin coating. These pans make flipping your crepes a bit more successful, but they don't produce the golden, crisp texture that I love in my crepes. Nonstick pans tend to be a little thinner and the temperature distribution is not quite as even as a more substantial cast-iron or steel pan.

SPECIALTY PANS

You may have purchased this book because that special someone gave you a crepe pan or an electric crepe maker, and it's time to put it to use. Or you may have decided you wanted to make your own crepes at home just like they do at your favorite crepe shop, so you want to buy a crepe pan of your own.

Although not essential for making crepes at home, these specialty pans may make your cooking experience a bit easier. Here are some pros and cons of popular options besides your traditional pans at home.

THE TRADITIONAL FRENCH CREPE PAN
Cook N Home 10.25-Inch Nonstick Heavy Gauge Crepe Pancake Pan Griddle

This type of pan has a nonstick aluminum surface, providing even heat conduction. I like it because it's relatively inexpensive and its low sides make flipping a bit easier. You do need to season this type of pan, so be sure to follow the instructions provided with the pan before you use it. These pans are also susceptible to rust if they're not dried thoroughly.

THE ELECTRIC CREPE MAKER
Proctor Silex 38400 Electric Crepe Maker, 13-Inch Griddle & Spatula

This electric crepe maker features a nonstick surface, eight heat levels for fine-tuned temperature control, and all the tools you'll need to cook your crepes. It's a good choice because it's inexpensive, portable, and easy to use. The downside is that it is not that easy to store.

THE NOVELTY CREPE MAKER
Moss & Stone 8-Inch Electric Crepe Maker, Pan Style, Hot Plate Cooktop

My customers would come into the shop and tell me about this miraculous new crepe maker. I couldn't imagine it, but then I watched a video about it, and it works. You heat the cooking element, then dip the curved surface into a pan of batter and it cooks up a crepe in seconds. It's speedy and fun, but it doesn't turn out crepes with that golden crusty texture I love so much.

PRO TIP: LOOKING FOR A CREPE MAKER?

When you're looking to invest in a pan, I would recommend getting a regular or nonstick pan no larger than 10 inches in diameter. It can get difficult to flip crepes in a larger pan. Make sure the handle is sturdy. If you choose a nonstick pan, make sure you also purchase a rubber spatula for turning that will not scratch the pan surface. When choosing an electric option, most are similar and cost less than $50. Just make sure the temperature can get to at least 400°F—otherwise, it's

*hard not to tear the crepes. If you are looking to save
space, I would recommend a pan, as it is easier to store.*

Beyond the Pan

Besides finding your favorite pan, there are several tools you'll need,
and others that would be great to have, when making your perfect
crepe.

ESSENTIALS

Baking pans or sheets: Some recipes will call for the crepes to be
assembled and then reheated in the oven. You will need a cookie
sheet or a baking pan to lay the crepes in.

Bowls: I recommend using a bowl with high sides, as the flour can
get messy when you're mixing in a shallow bowl. Make sure it is
plenty big, because you'll need to blend the batter vigorously. You'll
also need a separate bowl to mix the dry ingredients in before you
add them to the wet ingredients.

Crepe rake: This is a small wooden tool that comes with most
electric crepe makers. It pushes the batter around so it covers the
pan in a thin circle. You can make your own crepe rake with a ¼-
inch dowel. Cut the dowel into two 7-inch sections and drill a small
hole in the middle of one of the sections. Glue the other section into
the hole to form a T shape.

Cutting boards: Choose a sturdy cutting board to use when
chopping, shredding, and cutting.

Grater: Many recipes call for shredding cheese or zesting citrus, so
a grater with several sizes of grating surfaces can be very helpful.

Heat-resistant rubber spatula: If you are cooking on a nonstick surface, or even a cast iron or steel pan, a heat-resistant spatula is a wonderful tool. Just be sure your spatula is labeled as heat-resistant—you don't want melted rubber as your crepe filling.

Ladle: Once your batter is prepared, you'll want to deliver a consistent amount of batter to the pan with a ladle.

Long metal spatula: If you are not using a pan with a nonstick surface, a metal spatula is perfect for releasing and flipping the crepe.

Measuring cups: You will need to precisely measure your dry and liquid ingredients, so you'll need both a large glass measuring cup and an assortment of smaller measuring cups for dry ingredients.

Measuring spoons: Proportions are important, especially in the batter. Don't rely on eyeballing the ingredients.

Parchment paper or silicone baking mat: If you need to heat crepes on a baking sheet, it's very helpful to use parchment paper or a silicone mat so the crepes will not break when removing them from the pan.

Scale: Ingredients such as meats and cheeses are easier to measure accurately in ounces rather than by cups. So to make the recipes here, you'll also need a kitchen scale to measure many of the ingredients. Get a small, inexpensive digital scale. You should be able to find one online for under $20.

Sharp knives: Many of the recipes call for dicing or chopping the fillings. The easiest and safest way cut is using a sharp knife. A good paring knife is always handy to have, as well as a chef's knife, which has a wide, tapered blade for chopping.

Whisk: A whisk will help you thoroughly blend the flour into the batter.

NICE TO HAVE

Blender: A blender is great to have for mixing crepe batter. It will make the batter lump-free, but you must allow the batter to rest after blending for at least an hour to get all the air out. Otherwise, you will have bubbles in your batter.

Mixer: You can use a handheld or stand mixer for the batter as well, but again, you'll need to allow extra time for the batter to settle.

Wax paper/parchment paper: If your plan is to make crepes ahead of time and freeze them for later, it is helpful to separate the layers of crepes by placing a piece of waxed or parchment paper between each one.

A CREPE-FRIENDLY PANTRY

Leftovers are completely transformed when they're folded into a delicious crepe. You'll also save time and money by whipping up a few crepes to create an entirely new dish from yesterday's dinner. There are several ingredients you'll want to have on hand in your pantry or refrigerator to be sure you're prepared to make a batch of crepe batter: flour of choice, eggs, milk of choice, and butter, margarine, or oil. If you are looking for a sweet snack, cinnamon, sugar, chocolate, peanut butter, apples, and bananas will offer you many possible combinations. Need something quick and on the go? Any type of cheese or meat with avocado and tomato can turn a crepe into a tasty meal.

The Method

Making crepes is quite simple, but it can be very intimidating for many people. Rest assured, it is easier than you think. With the proper instructions, you can make a perfect crepe that will impress and delight your friends and family.

MAKING THE CREPE

1. Clear and organize your workspace. This is one of my strongest recommendations when cooking *anything*. An organized space makes cooking so much easier and reduces the risk of mistakes.

2. Reread your recipe and gather together all the ingredients and tools you'll need. There's nothing worse than finding that you are out of a crucial ingredient when you're in the middle of cooking.

3. Mix the dry ingredients together. When measuring any type of flour, make sure you spoon the flour into the measuring cup

and then level off the top with the back of a knife. If you just scoop it out with the measuring cup, you may be packing in too much flour, which will make your crepes gummy and thick. The same goes for other dry ingredients: Always spoon rather than scoop and level with a flat surface.

4. Mix the wet ingredients in a separate bowl.

5. Gradually add the dry ingredients into the wet ingredients, whisking or blending a little at a time to keep the batter from clumping.

6. If possible, let the batter sit in the refrigerator for at least 30 minutes to settle the bubbles. Otherwise, you may have small air holes in your crepes.

7. Heat your pan or crepe maker to medium-high heat. Once the surface is hot, spread your butter or oil on the pan, and wait until you see a light-brown bubbly foam from the butter, or the oil starts to pop. I usually spread the surface of the pan with a

zigzag shape of butter or a light coat of oil to just cover the bottom of the pan. Be more generous with your cooking oil on the first crepe of the batch; as you continue to cook, the pan will retain the oil.

8. Carefully measure out the recommended amount of batter and pour it into the middle of the pan or onto the surface of the crepe maker.

9. This step is very important! You won't have much time to spread the batter, so you need to act quickly before it cooks onto the surface of the pan.

    If you are using a standard pan, pick it up by the handle and roll the batter around the bottom of the pan with a clockwise motion of the wrist. Try to get the batter to spread evenly and reach the edges of the pan.

    If you are using an electric crepe maker, use your crepe rake to spread the batter. Place the rake as if it were the big hand on a clock, keeping one end of the rake in the center of the surface. Pull the batter toward you in a sweeping motion, swirling the batter out to reach the edges. Keep sweeping the rake until you get an even, thin coating on the surface of the pan.

10. Wait until the batter has no shiny spots before flipping. If there is a shiny (wet) spot, the batter is not cooked thoroughly enough.

11. Now for the flip: Once there are no shiny spots, carefully release the sides of the crepe from the pan by running a spatula under and around the edges of the crepe. This will prevent the crepe from tearing and makes flipping a breeze.

12. Next, take the spatula and wiggle it under the center of the crepe, moving from the edge to about three-quarters of the

way to the top. Carefully lift the entire crepe out of the pan or surface of the crepe maker and flip it back onto the uncooked side by turning your wrist and rolling it off the spatula.

If the crepe starts to slip off-center, just grab another spatula or carefully use your hand to guide it back into place.

13. Once the crepe has been flipped, you can add your favorite fillings. Start with the items that you want to melt, like cheese or chocolate. Layer other ingredients on top of one another to prevent them from spilling out when folding. When you see the edges getting brown, fold the crepe over the fillings and slip it onto a plate or platter.

Voilà! You've made yourself a delicious crepe.

Folding Techniques

Crepes can be folded inside or outside the pan. If you fill your crepe outside of the pan, you will most likely use your fingers to fold it. To fold crepes that are still in the pan, I suggest having a second spatula or an extra knife or fork to secure the fold in place. There are several folding techniques you can try.

1 The basic fold: Lay the crepe on a plate or clean work surface and spoon or lay the fillings down the middle. Fold one side of the crepe over the center, just enough to cover the filling, then fold over the other side, like a letter. The filling will still be visible at the top and bottom of the crepe.

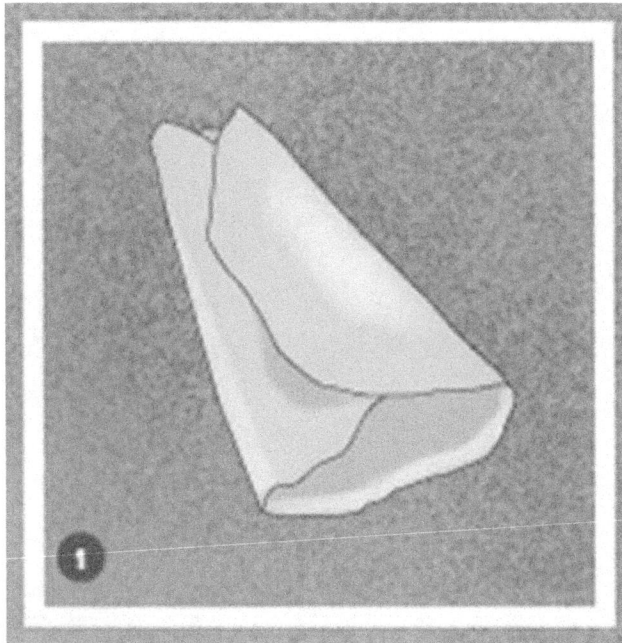

2 **The cone:** Lay the crepe down and spoon the filling into the center. Fold the bottom of the crepe halfway up to the middle. Then fold the sides across at an angle, creating a narrow triangle at the bottom with a wider top.

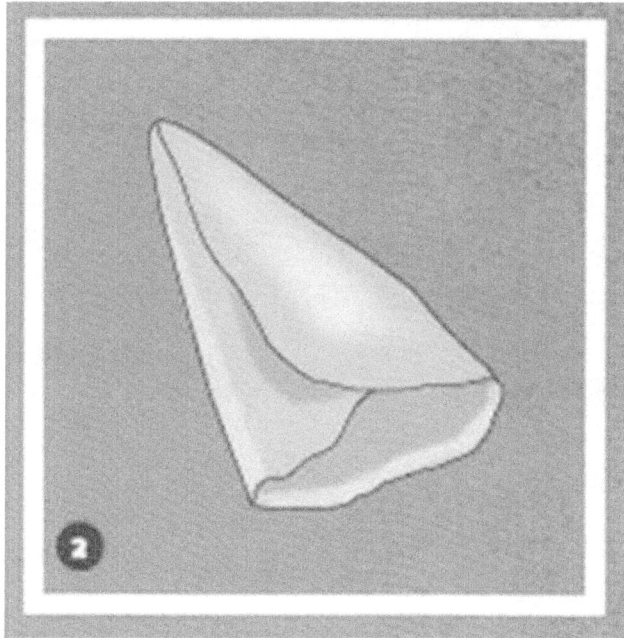

3 **The half moon:** This is the easiest way to fold a crepe. Fill one half of the crepe and lift the other half over the top to cover the fillings.

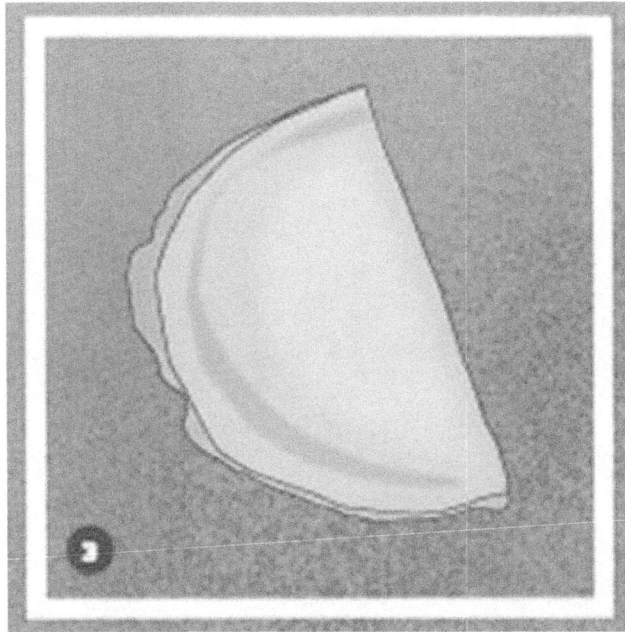

4 **The rectangle:** This fold is perfect for crepes that have multiple fillings or a messy sauce, preventing spillage from the ends. Lay the crepe down and place a spoonful or a layer of filling in the center. Fold both sides over the filling, as you would for the basic fold, and then fold the top and bottom as well to form a rectangle. Turn the crepe over so the folds are on the bottom and serve.

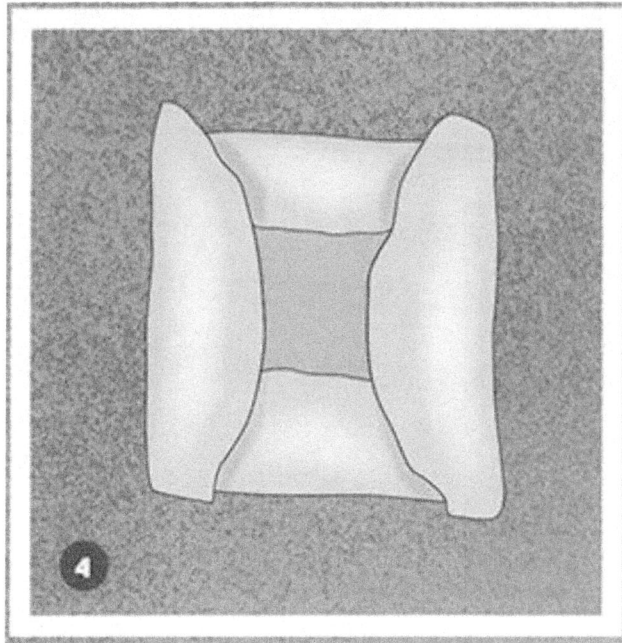

5 **The roll:** This shape is used mostly for dessert crepes. Lay the crepe down and spread the filling thinly over the entire crepe. Starting at one end, roll the entire crepe from one side to the other in a thin cylinder.

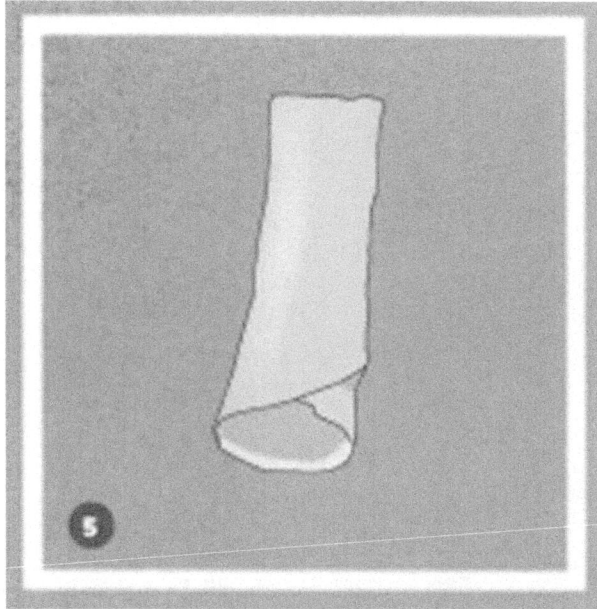

6 **The triangle:** Fill one half of the crepe completely, bringing the fillings to the very edge of the crepe. Fold the crepe in half, covering the filling. For a thicker crepe, bring the bottom third of the crepe to the bottom of the top third, then fold the top third over the other two thirds to make a triangle. You can also bring the bottom quarter of the crepe up to the top for a less layered and wider triangle.

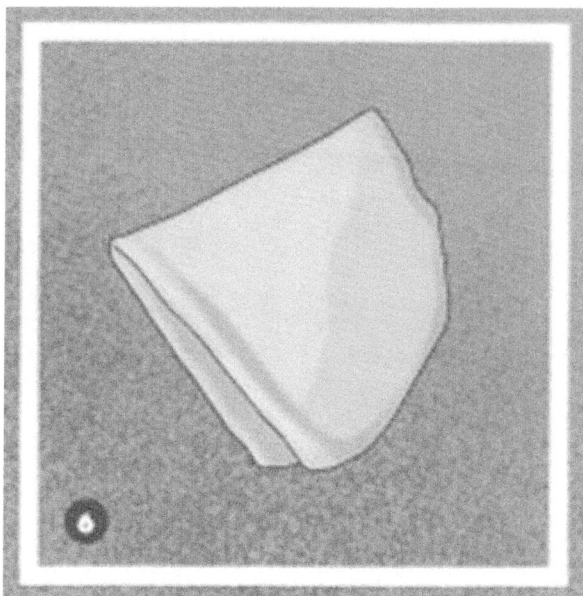

Troubleshooting

Here are some common issues you may encounter when trying to make your crepes and the best ways to solve them.

Why are my crepes too thick?

If your crepes are too thick, there are a few things that could be happening. First, make sure you are accurately measuring the flour when mixing the batter. If you scoop your measuring cup directly into the flour, you may be packing the flour down, adding more than the recipe calls for. Always spoon your flour into the cup and level off the top with the back of a knife. Another possibility is that you might not be spreading your batter quickly enough. If you pour your batter into the pan and do not spin out the crepe fast enough, it will become thick and chewy. It is always important to be ready to spread out the batter as soon as it hits the pan. Finally, if the batter itself is thick, it may be spoiled.

Crepe batter can last about five days in the refrigerator, but after that, it will become very thick, gummy, and sour.

Why do my first crepes always break and tear?

You are in good company if your first few crepes break and tear. I sometimes call them my "sacrificial crepes." To prevent tearing, you can try adding more butter or oil than usual for the first crepe. Your layer of oil or butter should coat the entire bottom of the pan, and even some of the sides. I like to use the end of a stick of butter and swirl it around the pan. Your first crepe will be a little crisper, but after that, you can just use a zigzag of butter or oil, and the rest of your crepes should turn out just fine.

Why aren't my crepes brown or crisp?

You may want to switch to a cast-iron or steel pan if you are using a nonstick pan. Sometimes the nonstick surfaces will not allow the crepe to brown evenly, and they may leave a pattern on the crepe. Try adding a bit more butter or oil and make sure you cook the crepe until you see a bit of brown around the edges.

Why do my crepes stick to the pan and tear?

You may be flipping your crepes too early. Be sure the surface of your crepe is no longer shiny and the edges are beginning to brown before you start to flip it. Also, make sure your edges are released from the pan by running a spatula around the entire crepe before attempting your flip.

Why are my crepes tough?

Try refrigerating the batter for at least 30 minutes. Gluten is formed when flour and liquids are agitated. This can produce a gummy effect, but refrigerating the batter after it's mixed relaxes the gluten and makes for light, airy crepes.

Why do my crepes break apart after I fold them?

Easy answer: They are packed with too much filling. You may want to use a larger pan to make a bigger crepe or put fewer ingredients on the crepe you have. Otherwise, your crepes will burst at the seams.

Why do my crepes always seem to burn?

You may not be using enough batter, which makes your crepes too thin and risks burning and disintegrating them when you try to flip or fold. Another problem could be that the temperature of the pan is too hot. The best way to know if the temperature is right is to drop some water or butter into the pan. The droplet should bubble but not smoke or sizzle. If it is smoking, the pan is too hot and will burn your crepe.

Why are there small air holes in my crepes instead of a smooth, flat surface?

When you mix or blend the batter, air gets worked in and makes it fluffy. If you try to use the batter immediately, this air will be trapped in the crepe and give it a cake-like texture. If you refrigerate your batter for at least 30 minutes to let the batter settle, the bubbles will disappear. You may see the batter start to separate, but this means it is ready to use. Mix it again lightly and begin cooking it once you have a smooth, silky batter.

Why are my crepes too thin and runny?

If you use too little flour or too much liquid in your batter, your crepes will be thin and hard to manage. The batter should be somewhat viscous, but not too much either way. One tip is to taste the batter after you have mixed it so that you always recognize the taste when making your batter in the future. If you have added too much or too little of something, tasting the batter will allow you to adjust it before cooking. You may also want to simply add more batter to the pan if your crepe appears too thin.

How do I keep my crepes hot if I am making multiple servings?

If you are preparing crepes for a crowd and want to serve them all at one time, place your crepes on a baking sheet lined with parchment paper and place them in the oven at 300°F. As you cook the crepes, add each finished one to the pan in the oven, which will keep them warm without making them soggy. Serve when all of the crepes are complete.

LEFTOVERS

Crepes are best fresh out of the pan, but you may want to make them ahead or save some extras that didn't get eaten. If you plan on using the leftovers within three days, you can store them in the refrigerator. Stack them on a flat surface, placing a piece of parchment paper or wax paper between each crepe to keep them from sticking together, then cover them in foil and keep chilled. If you want to save your leftovers for longer, you can use the same method of wrapping the crepes to freeze them for up to three months. When you're ready to use your frozen crepes, thaw them overnight in the refrigerator. Reheat leftover crepes in a pan over low heat or in a 300°F oven for about 10 minutes. They'll be nearly as delicious as the day you made them.

You can also save uncooked batter. Tightly seal the batter and place it in the refrigerator for up to five days or in the freezer for up to six months. Be sure to thaw frozen batter overnight in the refrigerator before cooking.

About the Recipes

There are recipes in this book for both main-course dishes and desserts, and the formulas for the batters cover every dietary preference. My recipes use a broad range of ingredients, including vegetarian, vegan, paleo-friendly, keto-friendly (in this book, the keto-friendly label has been applied to recipes that roughly meet the macros ratio of: 70 to 80 percent fat, 15 to 20 percent protein, and 5 to 10 percent carbs.), and gluten-free options. There are also several recipes designed for seasonal options, using fruits and vegetables that are fresh and available at different times of the year.

I've recommended batters and folds to go with each recipe, but you're always welcome to use your favorite batter to make the crepe of your choice. The combinations are virtually endless. Just be sure to pick the appropriate batter if you're cooking for someone with a specific dietary preference or need.

VE Vegetarian

VG Vegan

GF Gluten-free

KF Keto-friendly

PF Paleo-friendly

Chapter 2

CREPE BATTERS

The Quintessential Sweet Crepe
Savory Buckwheat Galettes
Sweet Gluten-Free Crepes
Savory Gluten-Free Crepes
Sweet Vegan Crepes
Savory Vegan Crepes
Sweet Keto-Friendly Crepes
Savory Keto-Friendly Crepes
Sweet Paleo-Friendly Crepes
Savory Paleo-Friendly Crepes

The Quintessential Sweet Crepe

MAKES: 8 (8- to 10-inch) crepes
PREP TIME: 10 minutes, plus recommended resting time of 1 hour
COOK TIME: 5 minutes
TOTAL TIME: 1 hour 15 minutes

VE

Close your eyes and imagine standing on a street corner in Paris while eating a crepe made from this simple recipe. There are only six ingredients, and all of them are most likely in your pantry or fridge at this moment. This is the perfect go-to recipe for an afternoon snack or delicious dessert, and you can use it for savory fillings as well.

2 large eggs
1¼ cups whole milk
2 cups all-purpose flour
2 teaspoons sugar
Pinch salt
Butter, for greasing the pan

1. Combine the eggs and milk in a blender and briefly mix to break up the yolks. Add the flour, sugar, and salt and mix thoroughly until there are no lumps in the batter. Scrape the sides of the blender and mix again until the batter is smooth. If possible, allow the batter to rest for 1 hour before cooking.

2. Place an 8- to 10-inch pan over medium heat. When the pan is hot, run a stick of butter along the bottom of the pan with a zigzag motion to coat.

3. Pour about ¼ cup of batter into the pan and spread using a

swirling motion to cover bottom of the pan. Reduce the heat to medium-low.

4. When the crepe no longer has any shiny spots, gently release the sides of the crepe using a rubber or metal spatula, then run the spatula up the middle and flip.

5. Repeat with the remaining batter. Fill, fold, and enjoy.

Troubleshooting Tip: *Make sure to measure the flour accurately by spooning it into a measuring cup and leveling off the top. Too much flour will make the crepes gummy.*

Per serving: Calories: 172; Total fat: 4g; Carbohydrates: 27g; Fiber: 1g; Protein: 6g

Savory Buckwheat Galettes

MAKES: 8 (10-inch) crepes
PREP TIME: 10 minutes, plus recommended resting time of 1 hour
COOK TIME: 5 minutes
TOTAL TIME: 1 hour 15 minutes

VE **GF**

The galette, or buckwheat crepe, which originated in Brittany, was the original crepe. It was not until hundreds of years later that white flour was substituted for the richer, nuttier buckwheat version. Galettes are delicious in both sweet and savory recipes, and also happen to be gluten-free. They can be a bit difficult to work with due to the absence of gluten to hold the crepe together, but they're well worth the challenge.

1¼ cups buckwheat flour
1 tablespoon sugar
Pinch salt
3 large eggs
1¼ cups whole milk
Butter, for greasing the pan

1. Mix the flour, sugar, and salt in a bowl and make a small well in the center. Add the eggs and half the milk to the well. Whisk together. Add the remaining milk and mix until you have a smooth batter. If possible, allow the batter to rest for 1 hour before cooking.

2. Spread some butter in a 10-inch crepe pan and heat over medium heat until it starts to smoke.

28

3. Pour about ¼ cup of batter into the pan, tilting until the base is coated in a thin layer.

4. Cook for 1 to 2 minutes, until the underside begins to brown and there are no wet spots on the crepe.

5. Release the sides of the crepe from the pan with a rubber or metal spatula and flip the crepe. Cook for another 30 to 45 seconds.

6. Repeat with the remaining batter. Fill and fold.

Troubleshooting Tip: *Make sure the bottom of the pan is totally covered with butter before pouring in the batter to keep the crepes from sticking.*

Per serving: Calories: 130; Total fat: 5g; Carbohydrates: 16g; Fiber: 2g; Protein: 6g

Sweet Gluten-Free Crepes

MAKES: 8 (8-inch) crepes

PREP TIME: 10 minutes, plus recommended resting time of at least 30 minutes

COOK TIME: 6 minutes

TOTAL TIME: 46 minutes

VE **GF**

This crepe batter has a gently sweet flavor and light texture and can be filled with either sweet or savory filling. It's especially important to measure the flour very accurately when you're preparing this batter, since gluten-free flours can be a bit harder to handle. It's best to use a nonstick pan, too.

2 large eggs
¾ cup whole milk
½ cup water
2 tablespoons melted butter
1 teaspoon vanilla extract
1 cup gluten-free all-purpose flour
2 tablespoons sugar
Pinch salt
Gluten-free oil spray

1. Place the eggs in a large bowl and blend. Add the milk, water, melted butter, and vanilla and blend. Then gradually add the flour, sugar, and salt.

2. Using a handheld electric mixer, mix for about 1 minute on medium speed, or until the batter is creamy with no lumps. If

possible, allow the batter to rest for 30 minutes before cooking.

3. Place a nonstick 8-inch pan over medium heat and coat with gluten-free oil spray.

4. Pour ¼ cup of batter into the pan and twirl until the batter is evenly coated on the bottom of the pan. Cook until the edges turn brown and no liquidy spots remain on the bottom. Release the edges from the pan with a rubber spatula and flip the crepe.

5. Repeat with the remaining batter. Fill and fold.

Substitution Tip: *You can make this recipe dairy-free by substituting almond milk and dairy-free butter.*

Troubleshooting Tip: *I recommend using a handheld electric mixer to prepare this batter, though you can still make do with a whisk and some elbow grease if you don't have a mixer on hand.*

Per serving: Calories: 136; Total fat: 5g; Carbohydrates: 19g; Fiber: 0g; Protein: 3g

Savory Gluten-Free Crepes

MAKES: 8 (8-inch) crepes

PREP TIME: 10 minutes, plus recommended resting time of at least 30 minutes

COOK TIME: 6 minutes

TOTAL TIME: 46 minutes

VE **GF**

These gluten-free crepes make a great pairing with any savory filling you choose. Feel free to jazz up the flavor of the batter by adding a pinch of your favorite herb or spice in the first step. For example, you can make a gluten-free <u>Reuben on Rye Crepes</u> *by adding some caraway seeds and filling with corned beef, sauerkraut, cheese, and dressing. It doesn't get better than that!*

2 large eggs
¾ cup whole milk
½ cup water
2 tablespoons melted butter
1 cup gluten-free all-purpose flour
¼ teaspoon salt
Gluten-free oil spray

1. Place the eggs in a large bowl and blend. Add the milk, water, and melted butter and blend. Then gradually add the flour and salt.

2. Using a handheld electric mixer, mix for about 1 minute on medium speed, or until the batter is creamy with no lumps. If possible, allow the batter to rest for 30 minutes before cooking.

3. Place a nonstick 8-inch pan over medium heat and coat with gluten-free oil spray.

4. Pour ¼ cup of batter into the pan and twirl until the batter is evenly coated on the bottom of the pan. Cook until the edges turn brown and no liquidy spots remain on the bottom. Release the edges from the pan with a rubber spatula and flip the crepe.

5. Repeat with the remaining batter. Fill and fold.

Troubleshooting Tip: *I recommend using an electric handheld mixer to prepare this batter, though you can still make do with a whisk and some elbow grease if you don't have a mixer on hand. Go with a nonstick pan as well, since this batter is a bit difficult to handle.*

Per serving: Calories: 122; Total fat: 5g; Carbohydrates: 16g; Fiber: 0g; Protein: 3g

Sweet Vegan Crepes

MAKES: 4 to 6 (8-inch) crepes

PREP TIME: 5 minutes, plus recommended resting time of at least 30 minutes

COOK TIME: 6 minutes

TOTAL TIME: 41 minutes

VG

This vegan crepe recipe is delicious and quick, and it works like a charm. The recipe is egg-free and cholesterol-free, making it a healthy alternative even if you're not vegan. This batter is usually paired with sweet fillings, but the flavor is neutral enough to use with savory fillings as well. The batter also keeps well—up to 10 days in the refrigerator and even longer in the freezer.

½ cup unbleached all-purpose flour

1½ teaspoons turbinado sugar

⅛ teaspoon salt

¼ cup soy milk

¼ cup water

1 tablespoon pure maple syrup

⅛ cup olive oil, plus more for greasing the pan

1. Combine the flour, sugar, salt, soy milk, water, maple syrup, and ⅛ cup of olive oil in a large bowl and mix thoroughly until the batter reaches the perfect consistency; not too thin, but not as thick as pancake batter. If it's too thick, add a bit more soy milk. If possible, allow the batter to rest for 30 minutes before cooking.

2. Heat an 8-inch pan over medium-high heat and pour a thin coat of oil to thoroughly cover the bottom of the pan. Once the oil starts to pop, add ⅓ cup of batter and swirl around the bottom to completely cover the pan.

3. Cook for 1 to 2 minutes, or until there are no spots of liquid on the crepe. Loosen the edges with a rubber or metal spatula and flip.

4. Cook for 1 minute on the other side, or until you see the edges start to brown.

5. Repeat with the remaining batter. Fill and fold.

Ingredients Tip: *Turbinado sugar is also sold as raw sugar. It is only partially refined and contains more of the natural molasses.*

Per serving: Calories: 147; Total fat: 7g; Carbohydrates: 18g; Fiber: 1g; Protein: 2g

Savory Vegan Crepes

MAKES: 8 (8-inch) crepes

PREP TIME: 10 minutes, plus recommended resting time of at least 30 minutes

COOK TIME: 6 minutes

TOTAL TIME: 46 minutes

VG

This batter makes a perfectly thin and chewy crepe with crispy, lacy edges. The crepes themselves aren't sweetened, but they can be paired with either sweet or savory fillings. They are great for a snack with fresh fruit, or you can melt various vegan cheeses in them with seasonal veggies for a filling meal.

1 cup all-purpose flour
½ teaspoon salt
½ teaspoon baking powder
1¼ cups soy milk
2½ tablespoons olive oil, plus more for greasing the pan

1. Combine the flour, salt, baking powder, soy milk, and 2½ tablespoons of olive oil in a blender and blend on medium speed until the batter is bubbly and all the lumps are gone.

2. Refrigerate the batter for at least 30 minutes before cooking.

3. Heat an 8-inch pan over medium-high heat. When it is hot, drizzle oil on the bottom of the pan to completely cover the surface.

4. Place ¼ cup of batter in the pan and swirl to evenly coat the

bottom of the pan. When the top is dry, loosen the edges with a rubber or metal spatula, then slide it under the crepe and flip. Cook the other side until it's golden brown on edges.

5. Repeat with the remaining batter. Finish with your favorite fillings and toppings.

Per serving: Calories: 115; Total fat: 5g; Carbohydrates: 14g; Fiber: 1g; Protein: 3g

Sweet Keto-Friendly Crepes

MAKES: 6 (8-inch) crepes

PREP TIME: 10 minutes, plus recommended resting time of at least 30 minutes

COOK TIME: 10 minutes

TOTAL TIME: 50 minutes

VE **KF** **GF**

If you are trying the keto lifestyle or you just want a new idea for a delicious, healthy meal, look no further. This low-carb recipe produces an easy-to-handle, versatile crepe that can enclose an endless variety of fillings. You'll never know that you aren't eating a crepe from a street stand in Paris!

3 ounces cream cheese, softened
½ cup almond flour
¼ cup unsweetened almond milk
3 large eggs
1½ tablespoons erythritol sugar substitute
⅛ teaspoon salt
Butter, for greasing the pan

1. Combine the cream cheese, almond flour, almond milk, eggs, erythritol, and salt in a blender on medium speed until they're thoroughly mixed.

2. Scrape the sides to make sure all the ingredients are incorporated, then set the batter aside in the refrigerator until any bubbles disappear, around 5 to 10 minutes. If possible, allow the batter to rest for 30 minutes before cooking.

3. Place a nonstick 8-inch pan over medium heat and add a small

38

zigzag of butter to the bottom of the pan. When the butter starts to bubble, pour in ¼ cup of batter, lifting the pan and swirling it so that the batter covers the bottom of the pan.

4. Once the crepe is no longer shiny and appears slightly brown around the edges, release the edges from the pan using a spatula. Then flip.

5. Repeat with the remaining batter. Fill and fold.

Troubleshooting Tip: *For best results, be sure your cream cheese is at room temperature, use a blender to mix the batter, and cook in a nonstick pan.*

Per serving: Calories: 151; Total fat: 13g; Carbohydrates: 3g; Fiber: 1g; Protein: 6g; Sugar alcohols: 3g; Net carbs: 0g

Macronutrients (per serving): 77% fat; 16% protein; 7% carbs

Savory Keto-Friendly Crepes

MAKES: 6 (8-inch) crepes

PREP TIME: 10 minutes, plus recommended resting time of at least 30 minutes

COOK TIME: 10 minutes

TOTAL TIME: 50 minutes

VE **KF** **GF**

These crepes are delicious and satisfying, and although they have no wheat flour, it would be hard to tell them apart from those served in the creperies in Paris. The crepe itself has a great flavor from the combination of cheeses in the batter, but you can spice it up more by adding a pinch of seasoning or minced herbs in step 1.

3 ounces cream cheese, softened

½ cup almond flour

¼ cup unsweetened almond milk

3 large eggs

¼ cup grated Parmesan cheese

2 teaspoons granulated sugar substitute, such as Swerve

⅛ teaspoon salt

Butter, for greasing the pan

1. Combine the cream cheese, almond flour, almond milk, eggs, Parmesan cheese, granulated sweetener, and salt in blender. Blend on medium speed until they're thoroughly mixed.

2. Scrape the sides to make sure all the ingredients are incorporated, then set the batter aside in a refrigerator until any

bubbles disappear, around 5 to 10 minutes. If possible, allow the batter to rest for 30 minutes before cooking.

3. Place a nonstick 8-inch pan over medium heat and add a small zigzag of butter to the bottom of the pan. When the butter starts to bubble, pour in ¼ cup of batter, lifting the pan and swirling it so that the batter covers the bottom of the pan.

4. Once the crepe is no longer shiny and appears slightly brown around the edges, release the edges from the pan using a spatula. Then flip.

5. Repeat with the remaining batter. Fill and fold.

Troubleshooting Tip: *For best results, be sure your cream cheese is at room temperature, use a blender to mix the batter, and cook in a nonstick pan.*

Per serving: Calories: 168; Total fat: 14g; Carbohydrates: 4g; Fiber: 1g; Protein: 7g; Sugar alcohols: 2g; Net carbs: 1g

Macronutrients (per serving): 75% fat; 17% protein; 8% carb

Sweet Paleo-Friendly Crepes

MAKES: 8 (8-inch) crepes
PREP TIME: 5 minutes
COOK TIME: 10 minutes
TOTAL TIME: 15 minutes

VE **PF** **GF**

This super-simple recipe is delicious and can be whipped up in minutes. Just combine the ingredients in a blender and cook—no need to rest in the refrigerator like traditional batters. The maple syrup adds a hint of sweetness to the batter, which pairs surprisingly well with savory fillings as well as sweet ones. This crepe holds together well, so it's also perfect for heavier protein fillings.

4 large eggs
1 cup unsweetened almond milk
1 cup almond flour
½ cup arrowroot flour
2 tablespoons pure maple syrup
1 tablespoon vanilla extract
Pinch salt
Olive oil, for greasing the pan

1. Add the eggs, almond milk, almond flour, arrowroot flour, maple syrup, vanilla extract, and salt to a blender and combine on medium for about 1 minute. Scrape the sides and blend again until the batter is smooth and creamy.

2. Heat a small amount of olive oil over medium-low heat in a nonstick 8-inch pan and swirl to cover the pan. Wait until the oil

is just about popping but not burning.

3. Measure ¼ cup of batter and pour it slowly into the center of the pan, then swirl the batter to thinly cover the bottom of the pan. Cook until all the liquid disappears, then carefully flip and cook an additional 30 seconds to 1 minute, just until the crepe is cooked through.

4. Repeat with the remaining batter. Fill or top the crepes and fold.

Substitution Tip: *You can substitute tapioca flour for the arrowroot flour, but other flour varieties may not work as well.*

Per serving: Calories: 171; Total fat: 10g; Carbohydrates: 14g; Fiber: 2g; Protein: 6g

Savory Paleo-Friendly Crepes

MAKES: 8 (8-inch) crepes

PREP TIME: 5 minutes, plus recommended resting time of at least 30 minutes

COOK TIME: 10 minutes

TOTAL TIME: 45 minutes

VE **PF** **GF**

Treat yourself to a tasty, healthy crepe that will add endless options to your paleo lifestyle. Low in fat, protein, and carbs, this crepe makes a guiltless treat. The arrowroot flour in the batter acts as a thickening agent and helps make a hearty crepe. You can fold it around your favorite proteins without it falling apart and it reheats nicely.

4 large eggs
1 cup unsweetened almond milk
1 cup almond flour
½ cup arrowroot flour
Pinch salt
Olive oil, for greasing the pan

1. Add the eggs, almond milk, almond flour, arrowroot flour, and salt to a blender and combine on medium for about 1 minute. Scrape the sides and blend again until the batter is smooth and creamy. If possible, allow the batter to rest for 30 minutes before cooking.

2. Heat a small amount of olive oil over medium-low heat in a nonstick 8-inch pan and swirl to cover the pan. Wait until the oil is just about popping but not burning.

3. Measure ¼ cup of batter and pour it slowly into the center of the pan, then swirl the batter to thinly cover the bottom of the pan. Cook until all the liquid disappears, then carefully flip and cook an additional 30 seconds to 1 minute, just until the crepe is cooked through.

4. Repeat with the remaining batter. Fill or top the crepes, and fold.

Substitution Tip: *You can substitute tapioca flour for the arrowroot flour, but other flour varieties may not work as well.*

Per serving: Calories: 159; Total fat: 10g; Carbohydrates: 12g; Fiber: 2g; Protein: 6g

Chapter 3

SAVORY CREPES

Red Beet Crepes with Spring Peas and Goat Cheese

Spinach Crepes with Mixed Mushrooms

Spinach, Blue Cheese, and Dried Tomato Crepes

Spinach and Artichoke Dip Crepes

Spicy Avocado Toast Crepes

Chickpea, Roasted Red Pepper, and Feta Crepes

Cuban Black Bean Crepes

Chili-Lime Black Bean and Corn Crepes

Savory Smoked Salmon Galettes

Red Beet Crepes with Arugula and Feta

Spicy Crab Salad Crepes

Jalapeño Chicken Crepes

Caprese Crepes

New Orleans Chicken Crepes

Almost Thanksgiving Crepes

Avocado-Beef Crepe Rolls

Classic Ham and Gruyère Crepes with Dijon Sauce

Reuben on Rye Crepes

Spicy Lamb and Chickpea Crepes

Italian Sausage and Pepper Crepes

Red Beet Crepes with Smoked Salmon

Spinach Salad Crepes with Warm Bacon Dressing

Spinach and Asparagus Crepes

Red Beet Crepes with Spring Peas and Goat Cheese

MAKES: 4 filled crepes
PREP TIME: 10 minutes
COOK TIME: 5 minutes
TOTAL TIME: 15 minutes

VE Recommended Crepe(s): Any sweet batter | Recommended Fold(s): Roll

This crepe is the perfect summertime dish. The spring peas give the crepe a crunchy texture, and paired with honey and goat cheese, it could even be served as dessert. This crepe is not only delicious, but a great way to impress your guests, especially if you use fresh spring peas from your garden.

4 ounces canned or jarred cooked red beets in natural juice, drained
Batter for 4 crepes
2 cups snap peas (about ½ pound)
4 ounces goat cheese
Butter, for greasing the pan
1 bunch watercress
2 tablespoons honey
Pinch salt
Pinch freshly ground black pepper

1. Mix the beets in a blender or food processor, adding a bit of the juice to make it more liquid. Once blended, fold the beets into the batter and stir until it is a consistent pink color.

2. Rinse the peas. Cut off the ends and pull the string on each pod

to open the pod in half.

3. Crumble the goat cheese.

4. Cook crepe in pan. Use a bit of extra butter to keep the crepe from sticking. Be careful not to overcook in order to keep the color pink rather than brownish.

5. Assemble each crepe by placing 6 snap peas in the center third of each crepe. Top with a handful of watercress and 1 ounce of goat cheese.

6. Drizzle with honey, then add salt and pepper.

7. Fold the sides into the middle third in a tube shape and serve.

Substitution Tip: *You can substitute feta for the goat cheese for a more savory filling.*

Per serving: Calories: 301; Total fat: 10g; Carbohydrates: 40g; Fiber: 2g; Protein: 13g

Spinach Crepes with Mixed Mushrooms

MAKES: 4 filled crepes
PREP TIME: 5 minutes
COOK TIME: 15 minutes
TOTAL TIME: 20 minutes

VE **GF** Recommended Crepe(s): Any savory batter | Recommended Fold(s): Triangle, Rectangle

Try something different by adding cooked spinach to your batter of choice—a delicious twist that adds nutrition and flavor to your dish. These elegant crepes can be served as an appetizer or add a hearty green salad to make them a meal. Adding the spinach to the batter does not change the cooking procedure for the crepe, so don't be intimidated to give it a try.

5 cups spinach
Batter for 4 crepes
2 teaspoons olive oil
2 shallots, finely chopped
2 garlic cloves, finely chopped
2 tablespoons butter
1 tablespoon chopped fresh rosemary
Salt
Freshly ground black pepper
5 cups sliced assorted mushrooms
4 tablespoons dry white wine
1¼ cups heavy (whipping) cream
2 cups grated Gruyère cheese

1. Rinse the spinach and place it in a large saucepan. Cover and

cook on low for about 5 minutes. Drain well, cool, and finely chop.

2. Stir the chopped spinach into the batter of your choice. Cook the crepes according to the batter instructions and set aside.

3. Heat the olive oil in a pan and fry the shallots and garlic, until tender. Add the butter and heat until it's bubbling, then stir in the rosemary, salt, pepper, and mushrooms. Cook and stir for about 5 minutes, until the mushrooms are soft and golden.

4. Stir in the wine and cream using a whisk and bring the sauce to a simmer.

5. Cover half of each crepe with the mushroom mixture and grated Gruyère cheese, then fold over.

Troubleshooting Tip: *Be sure to chop the spinach finely before adding it to the batter; otherwise, the crepes will be stringy and hard to cut.*

Per serving: Calories: 727; Total fat: 58g; Carbohydrates: 24g; Fiber: 4g; Protein: 28g

Spinach, Blue Cheese, and Dried Tomato Crepes

MAKES: 4 filled crepes
PREP TIME: 15 minutes
COOK TIME: 5 minutes
TOTAL TIME: 20 minutes

GF Recommended Crepe(s): Sweet Gluten-Free or any sweet batter | Recommended Fold(s): Triangle

This delicious crepe is an appetizer and main course all wrapped up in one. It's a great way to get the kids to eat their greens. This recipe is quick, easy and delicious. Feel free to add sliced chicken to make this a heartier meal.

2 tablespoons olive oil
2 cups baby spinach
4 ounces blue cheese
Batter for 4 crepes
1 (8-ounce) jar oil-packed sun-dried tomatoes
½ cup sliced walnuts
½ cup pistachios, shelled and sliced
Freshly ground black pepper

1. Heat the olive oil over medium heat. Add the spinach and cook for 2 minutes, stirring until all the spinach has wilted. Add the blue cheese and cook until melted. Remove from the heat.

2. Prepare a crepe with your batter of choice. Once flipped, cover one half of the crepe with one-quarter of the spinach–blue cheese mixture.

3. Slice the sun-dried tomatoes into bite-size pieces and add them

to the crepe. Add one-quarter of the walnuts and pistachios. Season the crepes with black pepper.

4. Fold in half, then in half again. Repeat with the remaining crepes and serve.

Ingredients Tip: *Make sure to use sun-dried tomatoes in oil; otherwise, they can be tough and hard to chew.*

Per serving: Calories: 587; Total fat: 43g; Carbohydrates: 38g; Fiber: 6g; Protein: 17g

Spinach and Artichoke Dip Crepes

MAKES: 4 to 6 filled crepes
PREP TIME: 5 minutes
COOK TIME: 40 minutes
TOTAL TIME: 45 minutes

VG **GF** Recommended Crepe(s): Any savory batter | Recommended Fold(s): Roll

This beloved appetizer dip, prepared vegan style, makes a mouthwatering filling for a savory crepe. Turn these crepes into a hearty meal by serving them with a salad or other vegetables. Just be sure to use fresh spinach rather than frozen for the perfect consistency.

½ cup finely diced yellow onion
1 tablespoon minced garlic
¼ cup water
10 ounces fresh spinach, chopped
1 (14-ounce) can artichoke hearts
1 cup plain dairy-free yogurt
½ cup unsalted cashews
1 tablespoon vinegar
Pinch salt
Pinch freshly ground black pepper
Batter for 4 to 6 crepes

1. Preheat the oven to 375°F.

2. Combine the onion, garlic, and water in a large pan over low heat. Simmer until tender. Add the chopped spinach to the pan a little at a time, then remove from the heat.

55

3. Chop the artichokes into quarters and drain well. Add them to the pan with the spinach.

4. Add the yogurt, cashews, vinegar, salt, and pepper to a blender and mix until everything is completely smooth. Pour the sauce over the spinach and artichoke mixture.

5. Transfer the combined mixture to a medium baking dish and bake for 25 minutes. Let cool for 5 minutes.

6. Prepare the crepes according to the batter instructions. After flipping each crepe, fill it with the spinach mixture. Roll and serve.

Per serving: Calories: 331; Total fat: 15g; Carbohydrates: 42g; Fiber: 10g; Protein: 12g

Spicy Avocado Toast Crepes

MAKES: 4 filled crepes
PREP TIME: 15 minutes
COOK TIME: 5 minutes
TOTAL TIME: 20 minutes

VG **GF** **Recommended Crepe(s): Any savory batter | Recommended Fold(s): Rectangle**

Avocado toast has become a restaurant sensation, and for good reason—it's both healthy and tasty. This version takes it to the next level by adding a flavorful chickpea-spinach mash with bell peppers and jalapeños and replacing the toast with a much superior crepe. I recommend using a mix of red, orange, and yellow bell peppers in this recipe for a delicious pop of color.

2 bell peppers, seeded and cut into ¼-inch strips
Pinch salt
Pinch freshly ground black pepper
1 medium ripe avocado
3 cups spinach
¼ cup jalapeño pepper slices
1 tablespoon freshly squeezed lemon juice
1 (15-ounce) can chickpeas, drained and rinsed
Batter for 4 crepes

1. Preheat the oven to 425°F.

2. Place the bell peppers in a baking pan and season with salt and pepper. Bake until brown, about 10 minutes.

3. Place the avocado, spinach, jalapeño, lemon juice, and salt and

pepper to taste in a food processor or blender and blend until smooth. You may need to scrape the spinach from the sides a few times to thoroughly blend the mixture. Transfer to a large bowl.

4. Add the chickpeas to the mixture and mash with a fork until no whole chickpeas remain and you have a thick, chunky texture.

5. Prepare a crepe as instructed in the batter recipe. While the just-cooked crepe is still in the pan, spread one-quarter of the avocado mixture in the middle, then fold in the sides to create a rectangle. Repeat with the remaining crepes and serve.

Ingredients Tip: *Make sure your avocado is fully ripe. If not, you'll have trouble mashing it, and it may even make the filling taste bitter.*

Per serving: Calories: 362; Total fat: 15g; Carbohydrates: 48g; Fiber: 11g; Protein: 12g

Chickpea, Roasted Red Pepper, and Feta Crepes

MAKES: 4 filled crepes
PREP TIME: 10 minutes
COOK TIME: 5 minutes
TOTAL TIME: 15 minutes

VG **GF** Recommended Crepe(s): Savory Vegan or any savory batter | Recommended Fold(s): Rectangle

This Greek-inspired crepe makes an excellent lunch or dinner when served with a fresh salad. It is filling, easy to make, and very adaptable. Feel free to experiment with adding a host of other ingredients such as tomatoes, cucumbers, or capers.

1 (14-ounce) can chickpeas, drained and rinsed
½ cup pitted and chopped black olives
¼ teaspoon ground cumin
Batter for 4 crepes
1½ cups sliced roasted red peppers
1 cup feta cheese crumbles
1 tablespoon extra-virgin olive oil
¼ cup chopped fresh basil

1. Place the chickpeas in a large bowl and mash them with the back of a spoon or a potato masher, keeping them semi-formed, not pulverized.

2. Add the olives and cumin and mix thoroughly.

3. Prepare the crepes according to the batter instructions.

4. Place the crepes on plates, then divide and layer the chickpea mixture, red peppers, and feta on half of each crepe. Drizzle with the olive oil and sprinkle with basil. Fold the other half of the crepe over the filling, then fold again and serve.

Ingredients Tip: *Try garnishing these crepes with sliced avocado and another sprinkle of fresh basil.*

Per serving: Calories: 379; Total fat: 18g; Carbohydrates: 39g; Fiber: 8g; Protein: 15g

Cuban Black Bean Crepes

MAKES: 6 filled crepes
PREP TIME: 20 minutes
COOK TIME: 5 minutes
TOTAL TIME: 25 minutes

VG **GF** Recommended Crepe(s): Any savory batter | Recommended Fold(s): Rectangle

This vegan crepe is stuffed with classic Cuban black beans and tastes absolutely incredible. It's a simple meal but delicious and healthy—and gluten-free, as well. I recommend topping these crepes with vegan cheese, avocado, cilantro, and a sprinkle of fresh lime juice. I love them for a quick breakfast on the run, but they're also great for lunch and dinner.

¾ **cup water, divided**
1 large red bell pepper, seeded and diced
½ **cup finely diced red onion**
4 large garlic cloves, minced
½ **tablespoon dried oregano**
1 teaspoon ground cumin
1 teaspoon fine salt
Pinch freshly ground black pepper
2 (15-ounce) cans black beans, drained and rinsed, or 3 cups cooked
1 (4.5-ounce) can mild green chilies
Batter for 6 crepes

Optional toppings

61

Sliced avocado
Vegan cheese
Chopped cilantro
Freshly squeezed lime juice

1. Combine ¼ cup of water and the bell pepper, onion, and garlic in a large pan over medium heat. Cook for about 8 minutes, stirring occasionally, until the veggies are tender.

2. Stir in another ½ cup of water and the oregano, cumin, salt, pepper, and black beans. Reduce the heat to medium and cook until all the water is cooked off. Stir in the green chilies. Remove from the heat and let cool slightly.

3. Prepare the crepes as instructed in the batter recipe. Then fill the center of each crepe with the bean mixture. Fold the sides in to form a rectangle, then top the crepe with whatever toppings you choose.

Troubleshooting Tip: *These crepes can be a little messy. Be sure to use the rectangle fold to keep the beans from spilling out.*

Per serving: Calories: 270; Total fat: 6g; Carbohydrates: 42g; Fiber: 11g; Protein: 15g

Chili-Lime Black Bean and Corn Crepes

MAKES: 4 filled crepes
PREP TIME: 5 minutes
COOK TIME: 10 minutes
TOTAL TIME: 15 minutes

VG **GF** Recommended Crepe(s): Savory Vegan or any savory batter | Recommended Fold(s): Roll

This recipe steals all the best taco fillings and folds them into a warm crepe with a good dose of lime juice. A cup of salsa adds even more flavor. Feel free to adjust the amount of red pepper flakes depending on the spice level you prefer.

2 (15-ounce) cans black beans, drained and rinsed, or 3 cups cooked
1 cup red salsa
½ cup frozen sweet corn
¼ cup water
2 tablespoons freshly squeezed lime juice
2 tablespoons mild chili powder
1 teaspoon ground cumin
1 teaspoon dried oregano
1 teaspoon salt
½ teaspoon red pepper flakes
¼ cup fresh cilantro, plus more for garnish
Batter for 4 crepes

1. Combine the black beans, salsa, corn, water, lime juice, chili powder, cumin, oregano, salt, and red pepper flakes in a medium saucepan over medium heat.

2. Cook and stir well until the mixture is thickened, about 5

minutes. Add the cilantro and heat through for 1 more minute.

3. Prepare the crepes according to the batter instructions. After flipping each crepe, add the bean filling to the middle third of the crepe. Fold in the sides and slide the crepe out of the pan onto a plate. Top with a sprig of fresh cilantro.

4. Repeat with the remaining crepes and serve.

Per serving: Calories: 355; Total fat: 7g; Carbohydrates: 59g; Fiber: 17g; Protein: 20g

Savory Smoked Salmon Galettes

MAKES: 4 filled crepes
PREP TIME: 15 minutes
COOK TIME: 10 minutes
TOTAL TIME: 25 minutes

KF **GF** Recommended Crepe(s): Savory Buckwheat, Savory Keto-Friendly or any savory batter | Recommended Fold(s): Cone

With just a few easy ingredients, this savory dish will delight and impress your guests. This recipe is best with freshly made crepes rather than ones that are premade and reheated. (Salmon can make crepes soggy if it sits too long.)

1¼ cups thick sour cream or crème fraîche
4 sliced radishes
1 bunch arugula
⅓ cup snipped chives
Pinch salt
Pinch freshly ground black pepper
Batter for 4 crepes
12 ounces smoked salmon

1. Combine the sour cream, chives, salt, and pepper in a small bowl. Set aside for the flavors to blend.

2. Prepare the crepes as instructed in the batter recipe. Stack the prepared crepes on a plate and keep them covered with foil or place in warm oven.

3. When all of the crepes are finished, arrange the smoked salmon on each crepe. Place a spoonful of the cream mixture

on top of the salmon and then fold each crepe to sandwich the fillings. The best fold for this is a cone shape, placing the salmon in the middle and folding in the sides, but leaving the top open. Serve on a plate or wrap in paper for a fun and festive occasion.

Ingredients Tip: *You can use either fresh or packaged smoked salmon for this recipe.*

Per serving: Calories: 345; Total fat: 30g; Carbohydrates: 2g; Fiber: <1g; Sugar alcohols: <1g; Net carbs: 2g; Protein: 18g

Macronutrients (per serving): 78% fat; 21% protein; 1% carb

Red Beet Crepes with Arugula and Feta

MAKES: 4 filled crepes
PREP TIME: 15 minutes
COOK TIME: 5 minutes
TOTAL TIME: 20 minutes

GF Recommended Crepe(s): Any sweet batter | Recommended Fold(s): Triangle

You won't believe how impressive these rosy pink crepes look, and they taste even better. Adding red beets to the batter gives these crepes their beautiful color, and combined with feta cheese and arugula, the dish is nearly a work of art. Feel free to substitute goat cheese for feta. Either way, garnish with extra walnuts and sprigs of arugula to finish off your pièce de résistance!

4 ounces canned or jarred cooked red beets in natural juice, drained
Batter for 4 crepes
Butter, for greasing the pan
1 bunch arugula
2 cups feta cheese crumbles
2 tablespoons honey
¾ cup chopped walnuts
Dash salt
Freshly ground black pepper

1. Mix the beets in a blender or food processor, adding a bit of the juice to make it more liquid. Once blended, fold the beets into the batter and stir until it is a consistent pink color.

2. Cook crepe in pan. Use a bit of extra butter to keep the crepe from sticking. Be careful not to overcook in order to keep the color pink rather than brownish.

3. Once flipped, top with a handful of arugula, then ¼ cup of feta. Drizzle with honey and a sprinkle of walnuts. Season with salt and pepper.

4. Fold the crepe in half, then fold into thirds in a triangle shape.

5. Garnish with additional walnuts and arugula and serve.

Ingredients Tip: *To get your batter even pinker, you can add a few extra drops of beet juice.*

Troubleshooting Tip: *Don't use buckwheat crepes for this recipe, because the darker batter will distort the coloring.*

Per serving: Calories: 517; Total fat: 35g; Carbohydrates: 34g; Fiber: 4g; Protein: 21g

Spicy Crab Salad Crepes

MAKES: 4 filled crepes
PREP TIME: 10 minutes, plus optional resting time of 30 minutes
COOK TIME: 15 minutes
TOTAL TIME: 25 to 55 minutes

KF **GF** Recommended Crepe(s): Sweet Keto-Friendly or any sweet batter | Recommended Fold(s): Roll

I'm from Maryland and we love our crab cakes, but they may have met their match with these crepes. This flavorful crab salad wrapped inside the crepe of your choosing is so simple, yet it tastes like you've been slaving over it in the kitchen for hours. You can substitute lobster for the crab if you're feeling fancy, and I recommend using the sweet version of whichever batter you choose. Serve with a green salad and you have a perfect meal.

2 teaspoons Old Bay seasoning
Pinch salt
Pinch freshly ground black pepper
⅓ cup mayonnaise
1 tablespoon sriracha
1 tablespoon chopped fresh cilantro
2 cups lump crabmeat
Batter for 4 crepes

1. In a large bowl, mix the Old Bay seasoning, salt, and pepper into the mayonnaise. Make sure the seasonings are thoroughly blended in.

2. Add the sriracha and cilantro and mix again. Fold in the

crabmeat.

3. If you're not serving immediately, cover the bowl and place it in the refrigerator. When you're ready to serve place the mixture in a small heat-resistant bowl and warm it in the oven at 350°F for 10 minutes to take the chill out of the salad.

4. Prepare the crepes as instructed in the batter recipe.

5. Once flipped, drop 2 scoops of warmed crab salad on each crepe and gently pull over the sides to roll the crepe.

6. Repeat with the remaining crepes and serve.

Make-Ahead Tip: *For best results, let the crab mixture sit for 30 minutes to allow the flavors to blend. The salad filling can be made ahead of time, then heated as described in the recipe.*

Per serving: Calories: 331; Total fat: 27g; Carbohydrates: 3g; Fiber: 1g; Protein: 18g; Sugar alcohols: 0g; Net carbs: 2g

Macronutrients (per serving): 73% fat; 22% protein; 5% carbs

Jalapeño Chicken Crepes

MAKES: 6 filled crepes
PREP TIME: 10 minutes
COOK TIME: 4 to 8 hours
TOTAL TIME: 4 to 8 hours 10 minutes

KF **GF** Recommended Crepe(s): Sweet Keto-Friendly, Sweet Gluten-Free, or any sweet batter | Recommended Fold(s): Rectangle

Don't be intimidated by the long cook time; this simple crepe filling takes only 5 minutes to assemble and then a slow cooker does all the work for you. Add a few ingredients to the pot, turn it on, and several hours later you'll have the perfect filling for your crepes. Another 5 minutes and you have an amazing meal that everyone will devour. The chicken is creamy, spicy, and cheesy, and pairs perfectly with a crisp crepe.

2 pounds boneless skinless chicken breasts
1 teaspoon garlic powder
½ teaspoon salt
¼ teaspoon freshly ground black pepper
8 ounces cream cheese
1 (4.5-ounce) can diced jalapeño peppers, drained
1 cup shredded Cheddar cheese
Batter for 6 crepes

1. Place the chicken in a 4-quart slow cooker and season with the garlic powder, salt, and pepper. Add the cream cheese on top.

2. Cover and cook until the chicken is tender and done, about 6 to

8 hours on low or 3 to 4 hours on high.

3. Using two forks, shred the chicken while it's still in the slow cooker, then add the jalapeños and Cheddar cheese. Mix well.

4. Turn the cooker on high heat for 10 to 15 minutes.

5. Prepare your batter of choice. Once each crepe is cooked and flipped, fill the center with the chicken mixture. Fold into a rectangle for support and less spillage. Repeat with the remaining crepes and serve.

Per serving: Calories: 544; Total fat: 36g; Carbohydrates: 6g; Fiber: 1g; Protein: 47g; Sugar alcohols: 0g; Net carbs: 5g

Macronutrients (per serving): 60% fat; 35% protein; 5% carbs

Caprese Crepes

MAKES: 4 filled crepes
PREP TIME: 10 minutes
COOK TIME: 5 minutes
TOTAL TIME: 15 minutes

KF **GF** Recommended Crepe(s): Sweet Keto-Friendly or any sweet batter | Recommended Fold(s): Triangle

This crepe features all the amazing flavors of caprese, with fresh basil, tomatoes, and melted mozzarella cheese. It makes for a delicious savory main course, and it even fits into the keto diet with the appropriate batter choice. Even though this is a savory dish, I recommend using a sweet batter recipe, as the hint of sweetness enhances the flavors that much more.

4 Roma tomatoes, sliced
Fresh basil leaves
Batter for 4 crepes
3 ounces fresh mozzarella cheese, shredded
Freshly ground black pepper
Olive oil, for drizzling

1. Slice the tomatoes and tear the basil into small pieces.

2. Prepare the crepes with your desired batter.

3. Once each crepe has been flipped, fill one half with tomatoes, mozzarella, and basil. Season with black pepper and drizzle a small amount of olive oil over the fillings (too much will make the crepe soggy).

4. Fold the crepe in half, then fold again into halves or thirds. Repeat with the remaining crepes and serve.

Substitution Tip: *You can add chicken or vegetarian chicken to add more protein and make it a savory entrée.*

Per serving: Calories: 267; Total fat: 21g; Carbohydrates: 8g; Fiber: 3g; Protein: 12g; Sugar alcohols: 0g; Net carbs: 5g

Macronutrients (per serving): 71% fat; 18% protein; 11% carbs

New Orleans Chicken Crepes

MAKES: 4 filled crepes
PREP TIME: 15 minutes
COOK TIME: 25 minutes
TOTAL TIME: 40 minutes

GF Recommended Crepe(s): Any sweet batter | Recommended Fold(s): Rectangle

You'll feel like you've been transported to the French Quarter as you bite into this loaded crepe. It takes all the good stuff in a muffuletta sandwich and replaces the bread with your choice of crepe. This combination of fillings would be perfect in any crepe, but I recommend using a sweet batter to best complement the flavors.

For the olive salad filling

¾ cup pitted and chopped mixed olives
1 roasted red pepper, chopped
2 garlic cloves, minced
1 tablespoon drained capers
1 tablespoon red wine vinegar
1 tablespoon olive oil
1 teaspoon dried oregano
Pinch freshly ground black pepper

For the chicken filling

3 boneless skinless chicken breasts, cooked and shredded
4 slices provolone cheese
2 ounces sliced salami
4 ounces sliced ham

4 slices mozzarella cheese
Batter for 4 crepes

To make the olive salad filling

1. Combine the olives, roasted red pepper, garlic, capers, vinegar, olive oil, oregano, and pepper in a large bowl and set aside.

To make the chicken filling

2. On a baking sheet, divide the shredded chicken into four small piles. Top each with a slice each of provolone, salami, ham, and mozzarella. Broil until the cheese is melted, about 5 to 10 minutes.

3. Prepare a crepe as instructed but use a 10- to 12-inch pan. After flipping the crepe, layer it with one pile of the chicken mixture in the middle, then top with some olive salad. Fold into a rectangle.

4. Repeat with the remaining crepes, then serve.

Troubleshooting Tip: *These crepes have loads of fillings, which is why I recommend a larger pan.*

Per serving (Olive Filling): Calories: 219; Total fat: 18g; Carbohydrates: 6g; Fiber: 2g; Protein: 7g

Per serving (Chicken Filling): Calories: 519; Total fat: 34g; Carbohydrates: 5g; Fiber: 1g; Protein: 46g

Almost Thanksgiving Crepes

MAKES: 4 filled crepes
PREP TIME: 15 minutes
COOK TIME: 10 minutes
TOTAL TIME: 25 minutes

Recommended Crepe(s): Any sweet batter | Recommended Fold(s): Rectangle

This crepe is what I call true comfort food. It's great to serve around the holidays, but folks will love it all year long. Feel free to add some of your family's favorite Thanksgiving dish to the filling to customize your crepe. I love to crisp it up with some creamed cucumbers, but they can be omitted for a super-quick version. I recommend using a sweet batter for this recipe to complement the cranberry sauce.

1 cucumber
Salt
½ cup heavy (whipping) cream
⅛ cup vinegar
1 tablespoon sugar
1 (6-ounce) package instant stuffing
1 (14-ounce) can whole berry cranberry sauce
Batter for 4 crepes
12 ounces lean cooked turkey, sliced into strips

1. Peel the cucumber and dice it into small cubes. Drain on a paper towel with a dash of salt to help the cucumber dry.

2. Place the cucumber pieces in a medium bowl and mix in the cream, vinegar, sugar, and a pinch of salt. Set aside.

3. Prepare the instant stuffing as directed on the package. (You can make your own stuffing, but for convenience's sake, I am recommending instant.)

4. Open the cranberry sauce and break apart the jelly.

5. Prepare the crepes as instructed in the batter recipe.

6. After flipping each crepe, place a few strips of turkey in the center, then cover with stuffing, add a spoonful of cranberry sauce, and top with the creamed cucumber mix. Fold into a rectangle and serve.

Substitution Tip: *To make this recipe vegetarian, just swap out the turkey for any vegetarian substitute.*

Per serving: Calories: 728; Total fat: 29g; Carbohydrates: 81g; Fiber: 4g; Protein: 37g

Avocado-Beef Crepe Rolls

MAKES: 4 filled crepes
PREP TIME: 5 minutes
COOK TIME: 5 minutes
TOTAL TIME: 10 minutes

PF **GF** Recommended Crepe(s): Any savory batter | Recommended Fold(s): Roll

This crepe filling is a perfect fit for the paleo diet, but it also can be gluten-free if you use the right batter. It's easy to grab for an on-the-go snack or to serve as lunch or dinner. Packed with protein, it sticks to your ribs, and kids will love it as well. Feel free to eliminate the apple and use the keto-friendly batter for a keto crepe.

Batter for 4 crepes
4 thin lean roast beef slices
1 small avocado, mashed
1 cup coarsely chopped spinach
1 small apple, cut into 8 pieces
¼ teaspoon dried oregano
¼ teaspoon dried rosemary

1. Prepare the crepes as instructed in the batter recipe. Layer them on a plate and set aside.

2. To assemble, place a crepe on a smooth surface and add a roast beef slice. Top with one-quarter of the mashed avocado and spinach, along with 2 apple pieces. Sprinkle with oregano and rosemary. Starting at one end of crepe, carefully roll it into a wrap. Repeat with the remaining crepes and serve.

Make-Ahead Tip: *You can serve these crepes hot, or you can chill them in the refrigerator and serve them cold.*

Per serving: Calories: 389; Total fat: 19g; Carbohydrates: 27g; Fiber: 2g; Protein: 31g

Classic Ham and Gruyère Crepes with Dijon Sauce

MAKES: 4 filled crepes
PREP TIME: 5 minutes
COOK TIME: 5 minutes
TOTAL TIME: 10 minutes

GF **Recommended Crepe(s): Savory Buckwheat or any savory batter | Recommended Fold(s): Rectangle**

Although the ingredients are simple, this combination of melted cheese with ham and a touch of Dijon mustard, all surrounded by a crisp crepe, makes a delectable treat. It's no wonder this earthy, rustic crepe is a classic. Buckwheat crepes are excellent here, but other batters can be substituted. You can experiment with other cheeses as well, such as Cheddar, Comté, or even a smoked Gouda.

4 teaspoons crème fraîche
2 teaspoons Dijon mustard
Batter for 4 crepes
1 cup grated Gruyère cheese
4 thin slices good-quality ham (about 1 ounce)

1. In a small bowl, stir together the crème fraîche and mustard. Set aside.

2. Prepare one crepe as instructed in the batter recipe, up until the flipping step.

3. Once you flip the crepe, sprinkle one-quarter of the cheese over the entire crepe and lay a piece of the ham in the center.

4. As soon as the cheese starts to melt, fold the bottom, top, and then the sides of the crepe over the filling toward the center, making a rectangular package. Continue to cook until the bottom of crepe is golden brown. Slide the crepe onto a plate, seam-side down.

5. Spread one-quarter of the crème fraîche–Dijon mixture on the top. Repeat with the remaining crepes and serve.

Substitution Tip: *While Dijon is recommended, you can also use a honey mustard paired with a sweet batter for a sweet and savory combination.*

Per serving: Calories: 260; Total fat: 15g; Carbohydrates: 16g; Fiber: 2g; Protein: 15g

Reuben on Rye Crepes

MAKES: 4 filled crepes
PREP TIME: 5 minutes
COOK TIME: 10 minutes
TOTAL TIME: 10 minutes

GF **Recommended Crepe(s): Any savory batter |
Recommended Fold(s): Triangle**

*This hearty crepe is a delightful twist on the traditional
Reuben, and it's so tasty that you won't miss the bread. You
can make this a gluten-free crepe as well if you use the
buckwheat batter. It's great for lunch or dinner, and you'll find
that the caraway seeds completely transform your batter.*

Butter, for greasing the pan
1 teaspoon caraway seeds
Batter for 4 crepes
½ cup sugar-free Thousand Island dressing
8 ounces lean corned beef, thinly sliced
1 (15-ounce) can sauerkraut, drained
4 ounces Swiss cheese, sliced or shredded

1. Heat an 8- to 10-inch crepe pan over medium heat and spread
   with butter to cover the bottom of the pan. When the butter is
   sizzling, spread one-quarter of the caraway seeds in the bottom
   of the pan.

2. Gently pour a ladle of batter in the bottom of the pan over the
   seeds. Slowly swirl the batter around, trying to keep the seeds
   from clumping, until the batter covers the bottom of the pan.

3. When the crepe is golden on the edges and no longer has any

wet spots, flip it gently.

4. Spread one-quarter of the dressing over the entire bottom of the crepe, then layer one half of the crepe with one-quarter of the corned beef, sauerkraut, and cheese.

5. Fold in half, then fold in halves or thirds. Repeat with the remaining crepes and serve.

Troubleshooting Tip: *To ensure that the caraway seeds stick to the crepe, place them in the melted butter before pouring the batter over the top.*

Per serving: Calories: 391; Total fat: 18g; Carbohydrates: 31g; Fiber: 6g; Protein: 27g

Spicy Lamb and Chickpea Crepes

MAKES: 4 to 6 filled crepes
PREP TIME: 5 minutes
COOK TIME: 25 minutes
TOTAL TIME: 30 minutes

GF Recommended Crepe(s): Any savory batter | Recommended Fold(s): Roll

This delicious combination of lamb and chickpeas will make you feel as if you've been transported to Morocco. Close your eyes and imagine a slow-cooked tagine, seasoned with herbs and spices, wrapped in a warm crepe. These crepes are best when rolled and served immediately with fresh cilantro to garnish.

Batter for 4 to 6 crepes
1 tablespoon vegetable oil
1 pound lean lamb fillet, trimmed and sliced
1 red onion, finely sliced
1 teaspoon mild curry powder
1 teaspoon ground cumin
Pinch salt
Pinch freshly ground black pepper
1 (14-ounce) can chopped tomatoes
½ cup trimmed and halved okra
1 (14-ounce) can chickpeas, drained and rinsed
Chopped fresh cilantro, for garnish

1. Prepare your crepes as instructed in the batter recipe. Stack the finished crepes and set aside.

2. Heat the oil in a large saucepan and gently fry the lamb, onion, curry powder, cumin, salt, and pepper until the lamb is browned on all sides, about 5 minutes. Stir occasionally.

3. Add the chopped tomatoes and bring to a boil.

4. Add the okra and chickpeas, then cover and simmer until the lamb is tender, about 20 minutes. Add water if the mixture becomes too dry.

5. Place a portion of the mixture on each crepe, covering the middle third of the crepe. Roll both of the edges on top to form a cylinder shape, then top with cilantro.

Per serving: Calories: 436; Total fat: 18g; Carbohydrates: 37g; Fiber: 9g; Protein: 34g

Italian Sausage and Pepper Crepes

MAKES: 4 filled crepes
PREP TIME: 10 minutes
COOK TIME: 30 minutes
TOTAL TIME: 40 minutes

PF **KF** **GF** **Recommended Crepe(s): Sweet Keto-Friendly, Sweet Paleo-Friendly, or any sweet batter | Recommended Fold(s): Rectangle**

This crepe is a great comfort food for any season, and your whole family will love it. It's perfect for the keto diet, but it fits the bill for many other lifestyles as well. With the proper batter, it can be gluten-free and even paleo, if a very lean sausage is used. I prefer using a sweet batter in this recipe for a delicious combination of sweet and savory.

2 tablespoons olive oil, divided
1 pound mild Italian sausage links
1 medium yellow onion, sliced
2 garlic cloves
1 red bell pepper, seeded and sliced
2 cups diced plum tomatoes
1 teaspoon dried oregano
Pinch salt
¼ cup chopped fresh basil
Batter for 4 crepes

1. Heat 1 tablespoon of oil in a skillet over medium heat. Add the sausages and cook until browned. Transfer to a cutting board and set aside.

2. Add the remaining 1 tablespoon of oil to the same pan, then

add the onion and garlic. Cook until tender, about 3 minutes, then add the bell pepper and cook for another 3 minutes. Add the tomatoes, oregano, and salt and mix well. Increase the heat to medium-high and simmer uncovered for 5 minutes.

3. Slice the sausage into ½-inch pieces. Add the sausage and basil to the sauce, mixing thoroughly, then simmer on low for 10 minutes.

4. Begin cooking the crepes. After flipping each crepe, fill it with the pepper and sausage mixture, keeping any liquid in the mixture from pouring on the crepe.

5. It's best to fold this crepe into a rectangle to keep the filling squarely in the middle. Repeat with the remaining crepes and serve.

Troubleshooting Tip: *Be sure to drain the sausage well after cooking. Otherwise, it will make the crepe get soggy and break apart.*

Per serving: Calories: 419; Total fat: 30g; Carbohydrates: 14g; Fiber: 3g; Protein: 26g; Sugar alcohols: 0g; Net carbs: 11g

Macronutrients (per serving): 64% fat; 25% protein; 11% carbs

Red Beet Crepes with Smoked Salmon

MAKES: 4 filled crepes
PREP TIME: 10 minutes, plus 20 minutes to chill
COOK TIME: 5 minutes
TOTAL TIME: 35 minutes

KF **GF** Recommended Crepe(s): Any savory batter | Recommended Fold(s): Half moon

These beet crepes are beautiful and delicious. Beet juice gives these crepes their distinctive color (though be sure not to use the buckwheat batter for this one—it will be too dark!). Smoked mackerel is a wonderful substitution for the salmon, and regardless of the fish you choose, garnish with a lemon wedge.

12 ounces smoked salmon, skinned and flaked
1 tablespoon lemon juice
4 tablespoons sour cream, plus more to garnish
2 tablespoons mayonnaise
1 tablespoon chopped fresh dill
4 ounces canned or jarred cooked red beets in natural juice, drained
Batter for 4 crepes
1 bunch watercress
Lemon wedges to garnish

1. In a medium bowl, gently mix the smoked salmon with the lemon juice, sour cream, mayonnaise, and dill. Cover and chill for 20 minutes to let the flavors blend.

2. While that is chilling, finely grate the beets and add them to the crepe batter. Stir until the batter turns an even pinkish color.

3. Prepare crepes according to the batter instructions.

4. Assemble the crepes by placing a layer of watercress on one half of each crepe, followed by the salmon mixture. Fold the other side over to cover.

5. Garnish with lemon wedges and a dab more sour cream.

Ingredients Tip: *To get your batter even pinker, you can add a few drops of the beet juice.*

Per serving: Calories: 185; Total fat: 12g; Carbohydrates: 3g; Fiber: 1g; Sugar alcohol: <1g; Net carbs: 2g; Protein: 16g

Macronutrients (per serving): 58% fat; 35% protein; 7% carbs

Spinach Salad Crepes with Warm Bacon Dressing

MAKES: 4 filled crepes
PREP TIME: 15 minutes
COOK TIME: 5 minutes
TOTAL TIME: 20 minutes

KF **GF** Recommended Crepe(s): Sweet Keto-Friendly, Sweet Gluten-Free, or any sweet batter | Recommended Fold(s): Triangle

This delicious crepe is an appetizer and main course all wrapped up in one. It's a great way to get the kids to eat their greens alongside tasty bacon flavor. Though this recipe is low in calories and carbs, it's high in flavor. Chicken makes this a heartier meal.

8 slices thick-cut bacon
2 tablespoons bacon fat (reserved from cooking the bacon)
2 shallots, thinly sliced
2 portabella mushroom caps, sliced
2 tablespoons red wine vinegar
1 tablespoon erythritol sugar substitute
1 teaspoon Dijon mustard
12 ounces baby spinach
4 hard-boiled eggs, sliced
Freshly ground black pepper
Batter for 4 crepes

1. Fry the bacon in a skillet over medium heat until it's crispy, then drain it on a paper towel. Crumble the bacon and set aside. Leave 2 tablespoons of fat in the pan.

2. Fry the shallots in the bacon fat until they are golden brown. Add the mushrooms and sauté until they're soft and tender.

3. To make the dressing, start with the remaining bacon fat in the skillet and whisk in the vinegar, sugar substitute, and mustard. Heat until warm.

4. Place the bacon, shallots, mushrooms, spinach, and eggs in a large bowl and toss with the dressing. Season with pepper.

5. Prepare a crepe with your batter. Once flipped, cover the entire surface of the crepe with one-quarter of the spinach mixture. Fold in half, then in half again. Repeat with the remaining crepes and serve.

Ingredients Tip: *Feel free to heap on a good amount of spinach in the last step; it will wilt significantly inside the hot crepe.*

Per serving: Calories: 284; Total fat: 20g; Carbohydrates: 12g; Fiber: 3g; Sugar alcohols: 3g; Net carbs: 6g; Protein: 18g

Macronutrients (per serving): 63% fat; 25% protein; 12% carb

Spinach and Asparagus Crepes

MAKES: 6 filled crepes
PREP TIME: 20 minutes
COOK TIME: 20 minutes
TOTAL TIME: 40 minutes

VE **Recommended Crepe(s): Any sweet batter |
Recommended Fold(s): Roll**

*This springtime crepe makes excellent use of asparagus
season. Though it takes a bit more prep time, the béchamel
sauce can be made ahead to save time. Make this gluten-
free by swapping almond flour for the all-purpose flour in the
béchamel.*

1¼ cups milk
1 small onion, chopped
1 bay leaf
Batter for 6 crepes
3 tablespoons butter, divided
¼ cup all-purpose flour
Salt
Freshly ground black pepper
24 asparagus spears, trimmed
8 ounces spinach
½ cup grated Cheddar cheese

1. Cook the milk, onion, and bay leaf in a saucepan over medium
   heat until it begins to boil. Take off the heat and let rest for 20
   minutes. Strain and set aside.

2. Prepare the crepes as instructed in the batter recipe and set
   aside.

3. To make the sauce, place 2 tablespoons of butter in a saucepan over low heat. When the butter is melted, whisk in the flour and cook for 1 minute. Take off the heat and gradually whisk in the infused milk until thoroughly combined. Return the pan to low heat and continue stirring until the sauce has thickened. Bring to a boil and then simmer for 2 minutes. Season with salt and pepper. Set aside.

4. Bring a large pan of water to a boil and blanch the asparagus for 2 minutes. Drain and pat dry.

5. In the same pan, melt 1 tablespoon of butter over medium-high heat and sauté the spinach until it's wilted. Set aside.

6. Assemble each crepe by placing 4 asparagus spears in the center, topping with spinach, then rolling the crepe. Once rolled, place all the crepes on a baking pan. Cover with the sauce and grated cheese and broil on high 8 to 10 minutes. Serve immediately.

Troubleshooting Tip: *Be careful not to overcook the asparagus or it will become soggy and stringy in the crepe.*

Per serving: Calories: 155; Total fat: 10g; Carbohydrates: 12g; Fiber: 3g; Protein: 7g

Chapter 4

SWEET CREPES

Lemon and Sugar Crepes

Lemon Bar Crepes

Crepes Suzette

Key Lime Crepes

Secret Ingredient Key Lime Crepes

Peach Cobbler Crepes

Braised Cherry Crepes

Apple Strudel Crepes

Apple-Berry Cream Crepes

Buttery Apple Crepes with Caramel Sauce

Toasted Coconut and Papaya Crepes

Banana, Chocolate, and Butterscotch Crepes

Banana and Hazelnut Spread Crepes

Pumpkin Pie Crepes

Crème Brûlée and Raspberry Crepes

Marshmallow Fluff and Strawberry Crepes

Peanut Butter Mousse Crepes

Kentucky Pecan Crepes

Baklava Crepes

Roasted Almond Butter and Chocolate Crepes

Crepes with Chocolate Sauce and Coconut Cream

Chocolate Cheesecake Crepes

Chocolate Espresso Fudge Crepes

Lemon and Sugar Crepes

MAKES: 4 filled crepes
PREP TIME: 5 minutes
COOK TIME: 5 minutes
TOTAL TIME: 10 minutes

VE **GF** Recommended Crepe(s): Any sweet batter | Recommended Fold(s): Rectangle

This classic crepe, so simple yet so very delicious, is a great recipe to start with. In fact, this was the first crepe I ever tried, on a freezing cold day in Paris. It warmed and nourished me unlike anything I'd ever had before, and it will always be one of my very favorites.

Batter for 4 crepes
4 teaspoons butter
2 lemons, cut in half
2 tablespoons granulated or confectioners' sugar

1. Prepare the crepes according to the batter instructions. Be sure to butter or oil the bottom of the pan generously, as you will want this to be a crispy crepe.

2. Once you flip each crepe, squeeze half a lemon over the entire surface of the crepe. Remove any seeds that may fall onto the crepe, then sprinkle with about 2 teaspoons of sugar. Fold the crepe immediately, as the lemon juice and sugar will heat up very quickly.

3. Repeat with the remaining crepes and serve.

Substitution Tip: *These crepes can be made to suit every type of dietary need. Make them keto-friendly by swapping out the sugar for erythritol sugar substitute or paleo by using pure maple syrup. They can also be vegan if you use margarine or dairy-free butter instead of regular butter.*

Troubleshooting Tip: *Be very careful when serving, as the lemon juice and sugar filling can get quite hot!*

Per serving: Calories: 206; Total fat: 17g; Carbohydrates: 9g; Fiber: 1g; Protein: 6g

Lemon Bar Crepes

MAKES: 4 to 6 filled crepes
PREP TIME: 10 minutes
COOK TIME: 30 minutes
TOTAL TIME: 40 minutes

VE **KF** **GF** **Recommended Crepe(s): Sweet Keto-Friendly, Sweet Vegan, or any sweet batter | Recommended Fold(s): Basic, Roll**

Lemon bars have always been one of my favorite desserts. With this tangy crepe recipe, I take out the crust and add a crepe to surround the lemon filling. Perfect for those following the keto program, these crepes can be made in advance and assembled in minutes. They can be eaten hot or even chilled—either way, they're sure to impress and delight your guests.

3 large eggs
¾ cup freshly squeezed lemon juice (from about 3 lemons)
¾ cup erythritol confectioners' sugar substitute, plus more for garnish
¼ cup almond flour
Zest of 2 lemons
Batter for 4 to 6 crepes

1. Preheat the oven to 350°F.

2. Crack the eggs into a large bowl and beat slightly. Add the lemon juice, sugar substitute, almond flour, and lemon zest and whisk until well combined and smooth.

3. Pour the lemon mixture into a lightly greased shallow baking

pan, such as a quiche dish or pie pan. Bake until the filling is set, around 25 minutes. Remove and let cool.

4. Prepare the crepes according to the batter instructions.

5. To assemble, fill the middle third of each crepe with a generous portion of the cooled lemon filling. Fold the sides over the middle third to form a cylinder and garnish with a sprinkling of the sugar substitute.

Per serving: Calories: 249; Total fat: 20g; Carbohydrates: 8g; Fiber: 2g; Protein: 12g; Sugar alcohols: 45g; Net carbs: 6g

Macronutrients (per serving): 72% fat; 19% protein; 9% carbs

Crepes Suzette

MAKES: 4 to 6 filled crepes
PREP TIME: 10 minutes
COOK TIME: 15 minutes
TOTAL TIME: 25 minutes

VE **GF** **Recommended Crepe(s): Any sweet batter |
Recommended Fold(s): Triangle**

*It doesn't get more classic than this! This French treat has a
rich history and makes the most stunning presentation:
Submerged in a buttery orange syrup, the crepes are
flambéed in front of your guests. Don't worry—you won't
need a fire extinguisher! The flames burn off by themselves,
leaving a rich, sugary coating on the crepes.*

**Batter for 4 to 6 crepes
4 tablespoons plus 1 teaspoon orange liqueur, divided
½ cup plus 1 teaspoon freshly squeezed orange juice, divided
8 tablespoons butter
½ cup extra-fine sugar
1 teaspoon finely grated orange zest**

1. When preparing your batter, add 1 teaspoon of orange liqueur
   and 1 teaspoon of orange juice to the mixture. Cook the crepes
   according to the batter recipe, stack on a plate, and set aside.

2. Place the butter and sugar in a saucepan over medium-high
   heat and cook until the sugar is melted. Stir in the remaining ½
   cup of orange juice, 2 tablespoons of the orange liqueur, and
   the orange zest. Bring the mixture to a boil and simmer until it's

syrupy, about 4 minutes. Transfer the syrup to a large frying pan.

3. Fold the crepes in half, then in half again, and arrange them in the pan in a wedge shape, bathing them with syrup.

4. Heat gently over medium-high heat for about 2 minutes, then pour the remaining 2 tablespoons of orange liqueur over the crepes, making sure the mixture is bubbling.

5. Carefully light the syrup in the pan with a long match and serve while flaming. To serve individual portions, remove a crepe from the dish and spoon some syrup over the top.

Troubleshooting Tip: *Serve these crepes in a dish with raised sides so the syrup doesn't spill over.*

Per serving: Calories: 467; Total fat: 36g; Carbohydrates: 25g; Fiber: 1g; Protein: 6g

Key Lime Crepes

MAKES: 4 to 6 filled crepes

PREP TIME: 5 minutes, plus 2 hours to chill

COOK TIME: 20 minutes

TOTAL TIME: 2 hours 25 minutes

VE **GF** **Recommended Crepe(s): Any sweet batter | Recommended Fold(s): Basic, Roll**

This deliciously tart crepe will transport you to the sunny Florida Keys. The lime filling pairs perfectly with sweet, crispy crepes and can be assembled in minutes. Just be sure to make the filling in advance so it has time to chill. These crepes can be served for a wonderful weekend brunch or as a light dessert for any lunch or dinner. Finish the crepes with a dollop of crème fraîche and a sprinkling of lime zest for a perfect presentation.

3 large eggs
1 (14-ounce) can sweetened condensed milk
½ cup freshly squeezed lime juice
Batter for 4 to 6 crepes
Crème fraîche, for serving
Lime zest, for garnish

1. Preheat the oven to 350°F.

2. Crack the eggs in a medium bowl, carefully separating out the whites and setting them aside.

3. Combine the yolks with the sweetened condensed milk and lime juice and mix.

4. Place the lime mixture in the bottom of a shallow baking dish, such as a quiche dish or pie pan. Bake for 15 minutes. Remove and chill in the refrigerator until set, at least 2 hours. You can also prepare the lime mixture in advance and refrigerate it overnight.

5. When you are ready to serve, prepare the crepes according to the batter instructions. Place a strip of the key lime mixture down the middle third of each crepe and fold the two sides over to form a cylinder. Top with a dab of crème fraîche and garnish with lime zest.

Ingredients Tip: *To add a bit of crunch to your crepes, try sprinkling some lightly crushed graham crackers over the filling before folding.*

Per serving: Calories: 531; Total fat: 25g; Carbohydrates: 60g; Fiber: 1g; Protein: 19g

Secret Ingredient Key Lime Crepes

MAKES: 4 to 6 filled crepes
PREP TIME: 10 minutes, plus 4 hours to chill
COOK TIME: 50 minutes
TOTAL TIME: 5 hours

VE **PF** **GF** Recommended Crepe(s): Sweet Paleo-Friendly, Sweet Vegan, or any sweet batter | Recommended Fold(s): Triangle

Key lime is a favorite, and this twist on the classic allows everyone to enjoy it. Avocados are the secret ingredient here, and when mixed with lime juice, they make a surprisingly delicious version of key lime pie filling. Adding beautiful candied limes makes these crepes a special treat.

For the candied limes

1 lime
½ cup water
¼ cup raw honey

For the filling

2 ripe avocados
½ cup freshly squeezed lime juice
½ cup raw honey
¼ cup coconut oil
⅛ teaspoon salt
Batter for 4 to 6 crepes

To make the candied limes

1. Thinly slice the lime. Combine the water and honey in a saucepan over high heat and bring to a boil. Add the lime slices and reduce the heat to medium-low. Gently simmer until the limes are translucent, around 40 minutes. Remove from the heat and allow the candied lime slices to cool completely in the syrup.

To make the filling

2. Peel and pit the avocados. Combine the avocados, lime juice, honey, coconut oil, and salt in a blender. Blend until smooth and let chill to solidify, at least 4 hours or overnight.

3. Prepare the crepes according to the batter instructions.

4. To assemble, place a generous spoonful of avocado filling over the center third of each crepe. Fold over the sides and garnish with the candied lime slices.

Per serving: Calories: 551; Total fat: 42g; Carbohydrates: 70g; Fiber: 10g; Protein: 10g

Peach Cobbler Crepes

MAKES: 4 to 6 filled crepes
PREP TIME: 10 minutes
COOK TIME: 15 minutes
TOTAL TIME: 25 minutes

VE **Recommended Crepe(s): Any sweet batter |
Recommended Fold(s): Rectangle**

*If you love peach cobbler, this recipe is for you. You get all of
the deliciousness of the peach filling and sauce, and the
crepe acts as the cobbler to surround this amazing dish.
Fresh peaches are best here, but if it's not peach season,
you can use frozen or canned peaches. Quick and easy,
these crepes make the perfect breakfast, snack, or dessert
for your friends and family.*

1 cup water
1 tablespoon freshly squeezed lemon juice
1 cup granulated sugar
¼ cup cornstarch
1 teaspoon vanilla extract
⅛ teaspoon ground cinnamon
**4 peaches, peeled, pitted, and chopped, plus additional
  wedges for garnish**
Batter for 4 to 6 crepes
Crème fraîche, for garnish

1. In a large saucepan, combine the water, lemon juice, sugar,
   and cornstarch over medium heat. Cook until thickened and
   bubbly, about 8 to 10 minutes, stirring often to keep the mixture
   from burning.

2. Remove the pan from the heat and stir in the vanilla and cinnamon. Add the peaches to the mixture and toss until everything is well combined. Allow the filling to cool to room temperature while you cook the crepes.

3. Prepare the crepes according to the batter instructions.

4. To assemble, spoon peach filling over the middle of each crepe, then fold the edges inward to create a rectangular package. Garnish with crème fraîche and as many wedges of fresh peach as you like on top.

Ingredients Tip: *For a spectacular touch, sliced almonds, powdered sugar, and thin slivers of orange peel are great additional garnishes.*

Per serving: Calories: 438; Total fat: 13g; Carbohydrates: 85g; Fiber: 3g; Protein: 7g

Braised Cherry Crepes

MAKES: 4 filled crepes
PREP TIME: 5 minutes
COOK TIME: 20 minutes
TOTAL TIME: 25 minutes

VE **GF** **Recommended Crepe(s): Any sweet batter |
Recommended Fold(s): Basic, Roll**

*Cherries are one of my favorite fruits, and when braised and
served inside a crepe, they are even better. This crepe
soaks up the luscious cherry sauce, and you'll want to
scrape up every last bite. It's best to use fresh pitted cherries
here, but in a pinch, you could substitute canned cherries by
rinsing off the sauce they're packed in.*

1 pound sweet cherries, pitted
2 tablespoons sugar
1 tablespoon cherry brandy or liqueur
1 teaspoon ground cinnamon
Batter for 4 crepes
½ tablespoon all-purpose flour
Water

1. Place the cherries in a medium saucepan with the sugar, cherry brandy, and cinnamon over medium heat. Bring to a boil, then reduce the heat and simmer uncovered for about 15 minutes.

2. Prepare the crepes according to the batter instructions and set aside.

3. When the cherry mixture is cooked and tender, remove the cherries from the juice with a slotted spoon and pile some on

the center third of each crepe.

4. Dissolve the flour in a little water to make a thin paste and whisk it into the warm cherry juice. Gently bring the juice mixture to a boil until it's thickened slightly, becoming smooth and rich. Remove the sauce from the heat.

5. Pour the sauce over the cherries on the crepes, then fold the crepes. Top with another drizzle of cherry sauce to serve.

Troubleshooting Tip: *These crepes are best served in a soup bowl since they can be a bit messy.*

Per serving: Calories: 260; Total fat: 13g; Carbohydrates: 29g; Fiber: 4g; Protein: 7g

Apple Strudel Crepes

MAKES: 4 filled crepes
PREP TIME: 10 minutes
COOK TIME: 10 minutes
TOTAL TIME: 20 minutes

VE **GF** Recommended Crepe(s): Any sweet batter |
Recommended Fold(s): Basic, Roll

Rich and perfectly tart, this fruity crepe is even better when served with a scoop of ice cream, yogurt, or vanilla custard. These crepes are surprisingly easy to make, and you can substitute your favorite fruit to personalize them for you or your family. Any way you make it, this crowd-pleaser is the ideal dessert for your holiday meal.

4 tablespoons butter
½ cup light brown sugar
3 honeycrisp apples, peeled, cored, and thinly sliced
Zest and juice of 1 lemon
⅓ cup golden raisins
⅓ cup pitted and chopped cherries
½ teaspoon ground nutmeg
½ teaspoon ground cinnamon
Batter for 4 crepes
Confectioners' sugar, for garnish

1. Melt the butter and brown sugar in a medium saucepan over medium heat until the sugar is completely dissolved.

2. Add the apples, lemon zest, and lemon juice to the pan and cook for about 5 minutes, constantly stirring. Stir in the raisins,

cherries, nutmeg, and cinnamon and cook for about 2 minutes more.

3. Prepare the crepes according to the batter instructions.

4. Place the warm crepes on plates and spoon the apple filling into the centers. Fold the sides in to cover the filling, creating a cylinder. Dust with confectioners' sugar and serve.

Substitution Tip: *To make it vegan, substitute a vegan-friendly margarine for the butter.*

Per serving: Calories: 482; Total fat: 25g; Carbohydrates: 62g; Fiber: 5g; Protein: 7g

Apple-Berry Cream Crepes

MAKES: 4 filled crepes
PREP TIME: 10 minutes
COOK TIME: 15 minutes
TOTAL TIME: 25 minutes

VE **PF** **GF** Recommended Crepe(s): Sweet Paleo-Friendly, Sweet Vegan, or any sweet batter | Recommended Fold(s): Half moon

This fruit-filled crepe is a must for everyone's dessert repertoire. The beauty of this traditional crepe is that you can change it up to suit your taste and the season with any fruit you like. This apple-berry version is especially simple and quick, since tart green apples and frozen berries are almost always available. It's a wonderful, warm dessert to enjoy all year long.

4 apples, peeled, cored, and chopped
¼ cup raw honey
3 tablespoons water
1 tablespoon coconut oil
Zest of 1 orange
1 teaspoon ground cinnamon
1½ cups fresh or frozen mixed berries
2 cups crème fraîche
1 sprig of mint
Batter for 4 crepes

1. In a large saucepan, combine the apples with the honey, water, coconut oil, orange zest, and cinnamon. Cover and cook over

medium-low heat, stirring occasionally, until the apples soften, about 5 minutes.

2. Add about three-quarters of the berries, cover, and cook for another 3 to 4 minutes, until the berries start to burst.

3. Prepare the crepes according to the batter instructions.

4. Add ½ cup of the crème fraîche to cover half of the crepe. Spoon the apple-berry mixture on top, adding the juice from the pan, which will be absorbed into the crepe. Fold into a half moon, then garnish with remaining berries and a mint leaf.

Ingredients Tip: *Try substituting the crème fraîche with the whipped coconut cream from the recipe for Crepes with Chocolate Sauce and Coconut Cream.*

Troubleshooting Tip: *If you're using frozen berries, you can add them to the pan in step 2 while they're still frozen. However, you may need to cook them for a few minutes longer.*

Per serving: Calories: 219; Total fat: 4g; Carbohydrates: 50g; Fiber: 6g; Protein: 1g

Buttery Apple Crepes with Caramel Sauce

MAKES: 4 to 6 filled crepes
PREP TIME: 10 minutes
COOK TIME: 20 minutes
TOTAL TIME: 30 minutes

VE **GF** Recommended Crepe(s): Savory Buckwheat or any sweet batter | Recommended Fold(s): Basic, Roll

Apples sautéed in butter and folded up in a crepe are delicious enough, but when you add caramel sauce, it's a heavenly treat. These are a favorite of mine in the fall when you have your pick of apples, but they're great any time of the year.

4 tablespoons unsalted butter, plus more for greasing the pan
4 firm, tart apples, peeled, cored, and diced into ½-inch pieces
¼ cup granulated sugar
1 teaspoon ground cinnamon
Pinch kosher salt
Batter for 4 to 6 crepes
Caramel sauce, for serving

1. Preheat the oven to 425°F.

2. Melt the butter in a large skillet over medium heat. When it's bubbling, add the apples and cook, stirring regularly, until they are just about tender, 7 to 8 minutes.

3. Sprinkle the apples with the sugar, cinnamon, and salt and continue to cook, stirring often, until the apples become tender, 3 to 4 minutes longer. Remove from the heat and let the apples cool.

4. Prepare the crepes according to the batter instructions.

5. Butter the bottom of a 9-by-13-inch baking dish.

6. Lay out the prepared crepes and spoon the apple mixture onto the bottom third of each crepe. Roll the crepes and place them seam-side down in a single layer in the prepared baking dish. Bake for 8 to 10 minutes.

7. To serve, lay a crepe on a dessert plate, drizzle a zigzag of your favorite caramel sauce over the top, and serve immediately.

Substitution Tip: *Try swapping out the apples for peaches during peach season—absolutely delicious!*

Per serving: Calories: 432; Total fat: 25g; Carbohydrates: 50g; Fiber: 4g; Protein: 7g

Toasted Coconut and Papaya Crepes

MAKES: 4 to 6 filled crepes
PREP TIME: 15 minutes
COOK TIME: 5 minutes
TOTAL TIME: 20 minutes

VG **GF** Recommended Crepe(s): Quintessential Sweet, Sweet Vegan, Sweet Gluten-Free, or any sweet batter | Recommended Fold(s): Rectangle

This amazing recipe takes the fruity flavors of a tropical summer vacation and wraps them all up in a coconutty crepe. When preparing your crepe batter for this recipe, you'll make one important change, substituting coconut milk for any other type of milk. You'll also add a sprinkle of shredded coconut while cooking your crepes for extra flavor. Close your eyes, bite into the crepe, and imagine yourself on a sunny island beach with your perfect dessert.

4 limes
¾ cup granulated sugar
¾ cup water
Batter for 4 to 6 crepes
Canned coconut milk (enough to replace the milk in the batter)
½ cup shredded coconut, toasted
2 large ripe papayas, peeled, pitted, and sliced
Coconut ice cream, for serving
Lime zest, for garnish

1. Pare the rind from two limes and squeeze the juice from all four limes into a small bowl.

2. Place the sugar and water in a small saucepan over medium-high heat. Add the rind and juice to the pan and boil rapidly for 10 minutes. Remove the rind from the lime syrup and set aside.

3. When making the crepe batter, replace the milk with an equal amount of coconut milk. If the batter is too thick, add a little water to thin.

4. Begin cooking the crepes according to the batter instructions. Just after you pour the batter into the pan and swirl it around to cover the bottom, quickly add a sprinkle of toasted coconut.

5. Flip the crepe and fill with pieces of papaya in the center, then add a spoonful of the lime syrup. Fold into a rectangle and repeat with the remaining crepes.

6. To serve, add a scoop of coconut ice cream to each crepe, drizzle with more lime syrup, and garnish with lime zest.

Troubleshooting Tip: *Be careful not to burn the coconut when toasting; it browns quickly.*

Per serving: Calories: 594; Total fat: 26g; Carbohydrates: 89g; Fiber: 9g; Protein: 9g

Banana, Chocolate, and Butterscotch Crepes

MAKES: 4 filled crepes
PREP TIME: 10 minutes
COOK TIME: 5 minutes
TOTAL TIME: 15 minutes

VE **GF** **Recommended Crepe(s): Any sweet batter |
Recommended Fold(s): Rectangle**

*This flavorful crepe is simple but sophisticated, making it the
perfect dessert for your fancy dinner party. The homemade
butterscotch has a dreamy texture and, combined with fresh
bananas, chocolate sauce, sliced hazelnuts, and a warm
crepe, it is an all-time favorite. Add a scoop of ice cream on
top to make it truly irresistible!*

1 cup butter
2 cups brown sugar
⅓ cup half-and-half
¼ teaspoon salt
1 teaspoon vanilla extract
2 large bananas
1 cup chocolate sauce
3 ounces toasted sliced hazelnuts
Batter for 4 crepes
4 scoops vanilla ice cream, for serving

1. In a small saucepan, melt the butter over medium heat.
   Gradually add the brown sugar, stirring constantly to make sure
   it does not burn. Lower the heat to medium-low and add the
   half-and-half, salt, and vanilla. Stir the butterscotch and remove
   from the heat. Let it set for 10 minutes.

125

2. Cut the bananas in half, then peel and slice them into ¼-inch pieces.

3. Prepare the crepes according to the batter instructions. After the crepe is flipped, place a quarter of the banana pieces in the center. Drizzle some of the homemade butterscotch and a ¼ cup of the chocolate sauce over the bananas, garnish with some sliced hazelnuts, and fold the sides of the crepe into the middle to form a rectangle. Remove from the pan and place on a plate. Repeat with the remaining crepes.

4. To serve, place a scoop of ice cream on each crepe and drizzle more butterscotch over the top.

Ingredients Tip: *For a butterscotch with more texture, try using only ¼ cup of half-and-half.*

Per serving: Calories: 1308; Total fat: 76g; Carbohydrates: 155g; Fiber: 6g; Protein: 11g

Banana and Hazelnut Spread Crepes

MAKES: 4 to 6 filled crepes
PREP TIME: 30 minutes
COOK TIME: 20 minutes
TOTAL TIME: 50 minutes

VE **GF** **Recommended Crepe(s): Any sweet batter | Recommended Fold(s): Triangle**

Hands down, this is almost everyone's favorite crepe. There's no need to buy the expensive jarred hazelnut spread when you can make your own with this delicious, simple recipe. This homemade version is a cinch to make, lasts for weeks, and will make you the most popular cook around. You can add pretty much anything you like to this crepe, but the most popular combination is serving it with sliced bananas.

¾ cup skinned hazelnuts
½ cup semisweet chocolate chips
⅔ cup sweetened condensed milk
1 tablespoon sugar
1 teaspoon vanilla extract
Pinch salt
Batter for 4 to 6 crepes
2 bananas, sliced

1. Preheat the oven to 350°F.

2. Place the hazelnuts on a baking tray and roast for 15 minutes, tossing frequently to toast the nuts on all sides.

3. While the nuts are roasting, melt the chocolate in a double boiler or microwave. If you're using a microwave, melt in 15-second intervals and be sure to stir in between until all lumps are gone.

4. Transfer the nuts to a food processor and grind until the mixture is pasty, around 1 minute. Add the condensed milk, sugar, vanilla, and salt and mix again. Scrape the sides often to thoroughly blend. Add the melted chocolate and mix again, blending until the mixture is uniform in color.

5. Prepare the crepes according to the batter instructions. Once flipped, spread the hazelnut mixture over the entire crepe and add a quarter of the sliced bananas to half of the crepe. Fold in half, then fold again in half or thirds for a triangular shape.

6. Repeat with the remaining crepes and serve.

Make-Ahead Tip: *You can store your homemade hazelnut spread in a jar at room temperature for up to five weeks.*

Per serving: Calories: 621; Total fat: 42g; Carbohydrates: 48g; Fiber: 6g; Protein: 16g

Pumpkin Pie Crepes

MAKES: 4 to 6 filled crepes
PREP TIME: 15 minutes
COOK TIME: 35 minutes
TOTAL TIME: 50 minutes

VE **GF** Recommended Crepe(s): Sweet Gluten-Free, Sweet Vegan, or any sweet batter | Recommended Fold(s): Basic, Roll

It doesn't have be Thanksgiving to enjoy these scrumptious crepes. In this recipe, I swap out crust for crepes, putting a new spin on the classic pumpkin pie. These crepes are sure to impress, and you can even make them a day ahead. Store the filling and crepes separately in the fridge, then assemble them when you're ready for a quick snack or dessert.

1 (15-ounce) can pumpkin puree
½ cup half-and-half
2 large eggs
⅔ cup erythritol confectioners' sugar substitute
1 teaspoon ground cinnamon
1 teaspoon ground nutmeg
1 teaspoon vanilla extract
¼ teaspoon salt
Batter for 4 to 6 crepes

1. Preheat the oven to 350°F.

2. Place the pumpkin puree, half-and-half, eggs, sugar substitute, cinnamon, nutmeg, vanilla, and salt in a large bowl and mix on high speed with an electric mixer until well blended.

3. Pour the mixture into a lightly greased shallow baking dish, such as a quiche dish or pie plate. Bake for about 35 minutes. When it's finished, a knife inserted in the center should come out clean. Remove from the oven and let the filling rest to firm up for about 10 minutes.

4. Prepare the crepes according to the batter instructions.

5. To assemble, pour a generous amount of pumpkin mixture on the center third of each crepe and fold over the sides to cover.

Ingredients Tip: *Try garnishing these crepes with a dollop of whipped cream and a sprinkle of ground cinnamon.*

Per serving: Calories: 270; Total fat: 19g; Carbohydrates: 14g; Fiber: 5g; Protein: 11g

Crème Brûlée and Raspberry Crepes

MAKES: 4 to 6 filled crepes
PREP TIME: 15 minutes, plus 3 hours to chill
COOK TIME: 5 minutes
TOTAL TIME: 3 hours 20 minutes

VE **GF** Recommended Crepe(s): Any sweet batter | Recommended Fold(s): Basic, Roll

This decadent dish pairs two French favorites, crème brûlée and crepes, in a single dessert. A rich, creamy brûlée filling is stuffed with raspberries and wrapped in a warm, crisp crepe. Since the filling is on the inside, there's no need for the intimidating kitchen torch to brown the topping. The brûlée cream can be prepared well in advance, making this perfect dessert even easier.

1 large egg
1 tablespoon all-purpose flour
2 tablespoons granulated sugar
1 tablespoon cornstarch
Pinch salt
1 cup whole milk
1 teaspoon vanilla extract
1 teaspoon hot water
Batter for 4 to 6 crepes
1 pint fresh raspberries

1. Combine the egg, flour, sugar, cornstarch, and salt in a small bowl and whisk until smooth.

2. Pour the milk into a saucepan over low heat and bring to a

simmer. Remove from the heat and slowly whisk the milk into the egg mixture.

3. Pour everything back into the saucepan over low heat and continue to whisk constantly until the sauce is thick and bubbly. Remove from the heat and stir in the vanilla and hot water. Refrigerate the brûlée cream until it's thick and cool, around 3 hours.

4. Prepare the crepes according to the batter instructions.

5. To assemble, spoon some brûlée cream down the middle third of each crepe. Cover with a generous portion of raspberries and fold the sides over.

Troubleshooting Tip: *Serve this filling on a cool crepe to keep the brûlée cream from melting into the crepe.*

Per serving: Calories: 248; Total fat: 16g; Carbohydrates: 16g; Fiber: 1g; Protein: 10g

Marshmallow Fluff and Strawberry Crepes

MAKES: 4 to 6 filled crepes
PREP TIME: 15 minutes
COOK TIME: 10 minutes
TOTAL TIME: 25 minutes

VE **GF** Recommended Crepe(s): Any sweet batter | Recommended Fold(s): Triangle

This warm crepe gently melts the marshmallow fluff within, mixing with the fruit filling for a delicious dessert or snack. Homemade marshmallow fluff is rich and creamy and not at all gummy, like the store-bought kind. If you really want to be decadent, you can add some chocolate and lightly crumbled graham crackers to the filling and make yourself a s'mores crepe—so delicious!

¾ **cup granulated sugar**
¾ **cup honey**
⅓ **cup water**
3 **egg whites**
½ **teaspoon cream of tartar**
1 **teaspoon vanilla extract**
Batter for 4 to 6 crepes
1 **pint strawberries, sliced**

1. Combine the sugar, honey, and water in a medium saucepan. Insert a candy thermometer into the pot and heat over medium-high heat.

2. While the sugar syrup is cooking, place the egg whites and cream of tartar in the bowl of a stand mixer (you can also use

an electric hand mixer here). Whip the egg whites to soft peaks.

3. When the sugar syrup reaches 240°F, remove from the heat and slowly add it to the egg whites while the mixer is on medium speed. When all the sugar syrup is incorporated, increase the speed and continue to mix until the fluff is thick and shiny, around 7 minutes. Add the vanilla and mix to incorporate.

4. Prepare the crepes according to the batter instructions.

5. To assemble, spread some fluff over half of each crepe, then top with strawberries. Fold over the other half, and then fold again. Garnish with another dab of fluff and a few more strawberry slices.

Per serving: Calories: 535; Total fat: 13g; Carbohydrates: 100g; Fiber: 3g; Protein: 9g

Peanut Butter Mousse Crepes

MAKES: 4 to 6 filled crepes
PREP TIME: 15 minutes, plus 5 minutes to chill
TOTAL TIME: 20 minutes

VE **KF** **GF** Recommended Crepe(s): Sweet Keto-Friendly or any sweet batter | Recommended Fold(s): Basic, Roll

Who doesn't love peanut butter? This rich mousse filling is incredibly easy to make and is ready to serve in just 20 minutes so you can spend more time with your guests and less time in the kitchen. This filling pairs beautifully with any sweet batter, and it's especially impressive topped with peanuts and shaved chocolate.

½ cup heavy (whipping) cream
4 ounces cream cheese, softened
½ cup natural peanut butter
½ teaspoon vanilla extract
½ cup erythritol confectioners' sugar substitute
2 tablespoons half-and-half
Batter for 4 to 6 crepes
Roasted salted peanuts, for garnish
Shaved sugar-free chocolate, for garnish

1. Whip the cream in a large bowl with an electric mixer for 2 to 3 minutes, until peaks form. Chill in the refrigerator.

2. In another large bowl, blend the cream cheese, peanut butter, and vanilla with an electric mixer until they're smooth and creamy. Add the sugar substitute and blend until it's thoroughly

mixed. Add the half-and-half and continue to blend until smooth.

3. Fold the cold whipped cream into the peanut butter mixture, gently mixing until the filling is firm. Refrigerate for 5 minutes.

4. Prepare the crepes according to the batter instructions and let cool.

5. To assemble, fill the middle third of each crepe with the peanut butter mixture. Fold into a cylinder and garnish with peanuts and shaved chocolate.

Per serving: Calories: 596; Total fat: 55g; Carbohydrates: 14g; Fiber: 3g; Protein: 17g; Sugar alcohols: 30g; Net carbs: 11g

Macronutrients (per serving): 83% fat; 11% protein; 6% carbs

Kentucky Pecan Crepes

MAKES: 4 to 6 filled crepes
PREP TIME: 10 minutes, plus 1 hour to chill
COOK TIME: 50 minutes
TOTAL TIME: 2 hours

VE **GF** **Recommended Crepe(s): Any sweet batter | Recommended Fold(s): Rectangle**

Pecan pie was just about my favorite dessert—until I discovered I could slip the nutty pie filling inside a crepe. This crepe is hard to beat: The rich, pecan-stuffed filling is the perfect consistency to tuck into a crepe, and it adds a new way to enjoy your favorite Thanksgiving confection. There is no really healthy option for this recipe, so just indulge yourself and enjoy!

1 cup light molasses
1 cup dark brown sugar
⅓ cup melted butter
1 teaspoon vanilla extract
½ teaspoon salt
1 heaping cup pecan halves
3 large eggs
Batter for 4 to 6 crepes
Whipped crème fraîche, for serving

1. Preheat the oven to 350°F.

2. Combine the molasses, brown sugar, butter, vanilla, and salt in a large bowl and mix well. Mix in the pecans.

3. In a medium bowl, slightly beat the eggs with a whisk. Fold

them into the molasses mixture.

4. Transfer the mixture to a lightly greased shallow baking dish, such as a quiche dish or pie plate. Bake for 45 minutes. Let the mixture chill in the refrigerator until set, at least 1 hour. You can prepare the pecan mixture the day before and refrigerate it overnight.

5. Prepare the crepes according to the batter instructions. After flipping, fill the center of each crepe with a generous portion of the pecan mixture. (If the mixture was refrigerated overnight, be sure to warm it in the oven first to remove the chill.) Fold in the sides to form a rectangle. Repeat with the remaining crepes.

6. To serve, top with whipped crème fraîche.

Make-Ahead Tip: *The filling is best made in advance to give it time to solidify. However, be careful not to reheat the pecan mixture too much or it will melt into the crepe and tear it during folding.*

Per serving: Calories: 569; Total fat: 32g; Carbohydrates: 63g; Fiber: 2g; Protein: 10g

Baklava Crepes

MAKES: 4 filled crepes
PREP TIME: 10 minutes
COOK TIME: 15 minutes, plus 10 minutes to chill
TOTAL TIME: 35 minutes

VE **GF** Recommended Crepe(s): Any sweet batter | Recommended Fold(s): Basic, Roll

Baklava, a renowned Greek dessert, is typically made with nuts, spices, honey, butter, and phyllo pastry. This tasty crepe promises half the work and 100 percent of the flavor. Crepes replace the tricky phyllo pastry, and you'll spread on the nutty filling and roll it all up for a layered treat that is perfect for dessert or as a snack for the entire family.

Batter for 4 crepes
5 ounces shelled unsalted pistachios, chopped into small pieces, plus more for garnish
½ teaspoon ground cinnamon
¼ teaspoon ground nutmeg
Pinch salt
½ cup sugar
½ cup water
¼ cup honey
1 teaspoon vanilla extract
4 tablespoons butter

1. Prepare the crepes according to the batter instructions. Stack them on a plate and set aside.

2. Combine the pistachios, cinnamon, nutmeg, and salt in a small bowl and mix.

139

3. In a small saucepan, combine the sugar and water over medium heat and cook until it's boiling. Reduce the heat and let the mixture simmer. Add the honey and vanilla and continue to simmer on very low heat for about 15 minutes, stirring often to prevent the sauce from burning. Remove from the heat and cool or chill.

4. Add the nut mixture to the sauce and stir.

5. Melt the butter over low heat in a small pan.

6. To assemble, brush each crepe with melted butter. Spread the nut mixture over half of the crepe and roll to form a cylinder. Garnish with extra pistachios and serve.

Troubleshooting Tip: *Be sure to let the nut filling cool and set for at least 30 minutes on the countertop or 10 minutes in the refrigerator before assembling the crepes. If not, it will be too runny.*

Per serving: Calories: 620; Total fat: 40g; Carbohydrates: 56g; Fiber: 5g; Protein: 14g

Roasted Almond Butter and Chocolate Crepes

MAKES: 4 to 6 filled crepes
PREP TIME: 10 minutes
COOK TIME: 15 minutes
TOTAL TIME: 25 minutes

VG **GF** Recommended Crepe(s): Sweet Vegan or any sweet batter | Recommended Fold(s): Triangle

This vegan version of an almond butter cup is super simple to make and will have everyone begging you for more. You'll roast the almonds to bring out their flavor and whip up a quick homemade spread that's far better than store-bought. After that, everything comes together in just a few minutes for a quick dessert or an indulgent snack.

3 cups raw, unsalted whole almonds
Batter for 4 to 6 crepes
6 ounces dairy-free semisweet chocolate chips or chopped vegan chocolate

1. Preheat the oven to 300°F.

2. Line a sheet pan with parchment paper and spread the almonds in an even layer over the pan. Roast for about 15 minutes.

3. Transfer the roasted nuts to a food processor and mix for a few minutes until the nuts turn into a paste, scraping the sides often to break up the clumps during the process. Keep mixing the

almond butter until it is completely silky smooth. Transfer to a small container or jar.

4. Prepare the crepes according to the batter instructions and let them cool for a few minutes.

5. To assemble, spread some almond butter over half of each crepe, then sprinkle with chocolate and fold.

Per serving: Calories: 585; Total fat: 48g; Carbohydrates: 26g; Fiber: 9g; Protein: 19g

Crepes with Chocolate Sauce and Coconut Cream

MAKES: 4 to 6 filled crepes
PREP TIME: 10 minutes, plus 40 minutes to chill
COOK TIME: 5 minutes
TOTAL TIME: 55 minutes

VE **PF** **GF** Recommended Crepe(s): Sweet Paleo-Friendly, Sweet Vegan, or any sweet batter | Recommended Fold(s): Basic, Roll

This recipe offers a naturally sweetened alternative to the classic chocolate crepe, perfect for the paleo lifestyle. The Sweet Paleo-Friendly Crepes batter is delicious here, and topped with a rich chocolate sauce and airy whipped coconut cream, these crepes will never make you feel like your dietary choices put any restriction on flavor.

For the chocolate sauce

¾ **cup raw honey**
½ **cup warm water**
⅓ **cup coconut oil**
1 cup raw cacao powder
⅔ **cup coconut cream**

For the whipped coconut cream

2 (15-ounce) cans coconut milk, chilled
2 tablespoons raw honey
Batter for 4 to 6 crepes

To make the chocolate sauce

1. Combine the honey, water, and coconut oil in a medium saucepan and bring to a boil over medium heat. Add the cacao and whisk until it's incorporated, then stir in the coconut cream. Remove from the heat.

2. Strain the chocolate sauce through a fine-mesh sieve and allow to cool.

To make the whipped coconut cream

3. Open the cans of coconut milk and pour off the liquid on top. Combine the solidified cream that remains and the honey in a large mixing bowl. Whip the cream using a stand mixer or a handheld electric mixer on high speed until soft peaks form. Chill for 40 minutes.

4. Prepare the crepes according to the batter instructions.

5. To assemble, drizzle the warm crepes with chocolate sauce, then spoon out some whipped coconut cream over the middle of the crepe. Roll the crepe and top with more sauce and cream.

Per serving: Calories: 678; Total fat: 68g; Carbohydrates: 44g; Fiber: 5g; Protein: 11g

Chocolate Cheesecake Crepes

MAKES: 4 to 6 filled crepes
PREP TIME: 20 minutes, plus 3 hours to chill
COOK TIME: 5 minutes
TOTAL TIME: 3 hours 25 minutes

VE **GF** Recommended Crepe(s): Any sweet batter | Recommended Fold(s): Basic, Roll

If you enjoy cheesecake, you will love this decadent crepe. Forgoing the traditional graham cracker crust, the crepe lends itself perfectly to the creamy filling. If you make the cheesecake filling in advance to give it time to chill, you'll have a delicious and sophisticated dessert in no time.

3½ ounces bittersweet chocolate, chopped
3 ounces white chocolate, grated
1 cup crème fraîche
½ cup light brown sugar
⅓ cup heavy (whipping) cream
1 teaspoon vanilla extract
Batter for 4 to 6 crepes

1. Melt the bittersweet chocolate in a double boiler or the microwave. Stir and let it cool, but not so much that it solidifies. Repeat with the white chocolate in a separate bowl.

2. Mix the crème fraîche and brown sugar until blended, then add the heavy cream and continue to mix until smooth. Divide the cream mixture into two small bowls and blend the bittersweet chocolate into one and the white chocolate into the other. Stir the vanilla into the white chocolate mixture.

3. Spoon a dollop of each mixture into one medium bowl and blend partially with a fork for a marbled effect. Continue adding the two mixtures in dollops and blending just until all of the filling is combined in one bowl and marbled. Chill for at least 3 hours to allow the mixture to firm up.

4. Prepare the crepes according to the batter instructions. To assemble, spoon a layer of the chilled mixture onto the middle third of the crepe. Pull the sides over the crepe to fold into a cylinder.

Troubleshooting Tip: *This cheesecake filling is best served on a cool crepe. If the crepe is too hot, it will melt the filling.*

Per serving: Calories: 424; Total fat: 29g; Carbohydrates: 32g; Fiber: 3g; Protein: 9g

Chocolate Espresso Fudge Crepes

MAKES: 4 to 6 filled crepes
PREP TIME: 15 minutes, plus 2 hours to chill
COOK TIME: 5 minutes
TOTAL TIME: 2 hours 20 minutes

VG **GF** Recommended Crepe(s): Sweet Vegan or any sweet batter | Recommended Fold(s): Triangle

These amazing crepes have everything you want in a dessert with their rich chocolate flavor, hint of espresso, and creamy fudge texture. Incredibly easy to make, the filling is best prepared in advance so it has time to chill. Feel free to use cashew butter in place of the almond butter, but just make sure it is the raw variety.

1½ cups dairy-free semisweet chocolate chips, plus more for garnish
½ cup canned coconut milk
3 tablespoons almond or cashew butter
1 teaspoon vanilla extract
½ to 1 tablespoon espresso powder
1 tablespoon cocoa powder
Pinch salt
Batter for 4 to 6 crepes

1. In a double boiler or the microwave, melt the chocolate chips with the coconut milk, stirring well until the mixture is smooth with no lumps.

2. Transfer the chocolate mixture to a food processor. Add the nut butter, vanilla, espresso, cocoa powder, and salt and process

for 2 to 3 minutes, or until it's completely smooth. Scrape the sides to ensure everything is thoroughly mixed.

3. Pour the fudge mixture into a bowl and chill for at least 2 hours or overnight.

4. Prepare the crepes according to the batter instructions.

5. To assemble, fill half of each crepe with the fudge mixture. Fold and garnish with additional chocolate chips or shaved dairy-free chocolate.

Make-Ahead Tip: *These crepes can be made in advance and refrigerated, or the chilled filling can be added to a hot crepe.*

Per serving: Calories: 416; Total fat: 33g; Carbohydrates: 21g; Fiber: 5g; Protein: 10g

Chapter 5

BEYOND THE CREPE

Rainbow Crepe Cake

Everything Crepes

Crepe Crisps

Crepe and Fruit Brochettes

Frozen Peanut Butter Cup Crepes

Ice Cream Crepe Cones

Bananas Foster Crepe Cake

Rainbow Crepe Cake

MAKES: 8 slices of crepe cake
PREP TIME: 15 minutes, plus 4 hours to chill
COOK TIME: 30 minutes
TOTAL TIME: 4 hours 45 minutes

VE **GF** Recommended Crepe(s): Quintessential Sweet, Sweet Vegan, Sweet Keto-Friendly, Sweet Paleo-Friendly

Sometimes you need a special dessert for a special occasion, and this is about as special as you can get. This cheerful crepe cake makes a perfect wedding cake, dinner party dessert, or children's party cake. The colorful layers are so festive but also incredibly easy to make. Just be sure to leave yourself enough time to cook all the layers and chill the finished cake overnight.

Batter for 24 crepes
Red food coloring
Orange food coloring
Yellow food coloring
Green food coloring
Blue food coloring
Purple food coloring
6 cups whipped cream

1. Evenly divide the batter into 6 small bowls. Place a few drops of red food coloring into one of the bowls and whisk until the batter is a rich, dark color. Repeat with each color in a different bowl.

2. Cook the crepes according to the batter instructions, starting

with the purple batter and repeating with all the different colors of batter. Let the crepes cool completely before layering.

3. Layer the crepes to create the cake. Start with a purple crepe and spread a thin layer of whipped cream between the crepes as you ascend through the rainbow to blue, green, yellow, orange, and red.

4. Coat the entire crepe cake with the remaining whipped cream, covering the top and sides to conceal the rainbow within. Let chill for at least 4 hours before slicing and serving.

Troubleshooting Tip: *Don't use buckwheat crepes for this recipe because the darker batter will distort the food coloring.*

Per serving: Calories: 764; Total fat: 72g; Carbohydrates: 12g; Fiber: 3g; Protein: 20g

Everything Crepes

MAKES: 4 filled crepes
PREP TIME: 5 minutes
COOK TIME: 5 minutes
TOTAL TIME: 10 minutes

VE **PF** **KF** **GF** Recommended Crepe(s): Any sweet batter | Recommended Fold(s): Triangle

An everything bagel packs so many flavors on the crust for a delicious combination. You can make an everything crepe as well, and it's a perfect breakfast treat for the entire family. You can also use this technique with whatever herbs or spices you like and pair it with the filling of your choice. My favorite with the everything crepe is the Reuben on Rye Crepes.

2 teaspoons poppy seeds
2 teaspoons sesame seeds
2 teaspoons onion flakes
½ teaspoon garlic flakes
1 teaspoon sea salt
1 teaspoon coarse pepper
Butter, for greasing the pan
Batter for 4 crepes
8 ounces cream cheese, softened

1. In a small container with a cover, combine the poppy seeds, sesame seeds, onion flakes, garlic flakes, salt, and pepper and toss to thoroughly mix.

2. Heat a skillet over medium-high heat and coat the bottom with

a layer of butter.

3. Add one-quarter of the seasoning mixture to the pan and sauté until the seasonings start to brown or the butter starts to bubble.

4. Add ⅓ cup of batter to the pan and quickly rotate to distribute the batter, trying not to let the seasoning clump to one side by not tilting the pan too steeply.

5. Flip the crepe, spread with cream cheese, and fold in a triangle. Repeat with the remaining batter and seasoning, and serve.

Troubleshooting Tip: *Try using whipped cream cheese in this recipe to prevent tearing the crepe.*

Per serving: Calories: 363; Total fat: 34g; Carbohydrates: 6g; Fiber: 2g; Protein: 10g; Sugar alcohols: 0g; Net carbs: 4g

Macronutrients (per serving): 84% fat; 11% protein; 5% carbs

Crepe Crisps

MAKES: 4 crepes
PREP TIME: 5 minutes
COOK TIME: 10 minutes
TOTAL TIME: 15 minutes

GF **Recommended Crepe(s): Any sweet batter**

This tasty snack was discovered as an experiment. One of my employees decided to cook some cheese and pepperoni on the crepe stone before pouring on the batter. To his surprise, it worked—and it was absolutely delicious. From there, we tried different combinations, some that worked and others that didn't. The recipe below is the best that we found, and it will impress the heck out of everyone. I would choose a sweet batter to enhance the sweet and savory combination.

1 tablespoon butter
4 ounces small pepperoni, sliced
4 ounces sliced salami, cut into strips
6 ounces Cheddar cheese
1 teaspoon dried oregano
1 teaspoon dried basil
1⅓ cups any sweet crepe batter

1. Heat a 10-inch skillet over medium-high heat and coat the bottom of the skillet with butter.

2. Once the butter starts to get brown and bubbly, place about 9 pieces of pepperoni and 6 slices of salami in the pan and cook until the edges of the pepperoni start to curl.

3. Sprinkle a handful of Cheddar and one-quarter of the dried oregano and basil over the top of the meat and cook until the cheese starts to melt.

4. Pour ⅓ cup of batter over the mixture and quickly spread. The cheese will keep the meat from moving around in the pan while you spread the batter.

5. Once the surface of the crepe is no longer shiny, flip the crepe and cook the other side until the edges are brown.

6. Repeat until you have used up all of the ingredients. Cut the crepes into small pieces and serve on a plate as a snack.

Troubleshooting Tip: *Cook the cheese until it's just golden brown before adding the batter.*

Per serving: Calories: 597; Total fat: 52g; Carbohydrates: 4g; Fiber: 1g; Protein: 29g

Crepe and Fruit Brochettes

MAKES: 8 brochettes (serves 4)

PREP TIME: 15 minutes

VG **GF** Recommended Crepe(s): Sweet Vegan or any sweet batter

This colorful creation is a wonderful and versatile treat. The brochettes can be passed as an hors d'oeuvre, served as a dessert at an event, or used as a tasty way to get kids to eat more fruit at children's parties. Feel free to swap out the suggested fruits with your favorites that are in season.

Batter for 4 to 6 crepes
12 large strawberries
1 ripe star fruit
1 ripe kiwi
1 pineapple
8 long bamboo skewers

1. Prepare the crepes according to the batter instructions and set aside to cool.

2. Roll the crepes and cut them into 1-inch-thick slices.

3. Hull and halve the strawberries. Slice the star fruit. Peel and cut the kiwi and pineapple.

4. Thread rolled strips of crepe and pieces of fruit onto the skewers, then cover and chill until it's time to serve.

Ingredients Tip: *Try serving these with sweet dipping sauces such as fruit yogurt or melted chocolate.*

Per serving: Calories: 288; Total fat: 14g; Carbohydrates: 38g; Fiber: 6g; Protein: 8g

Frozen Peanut Butter Cup Crepes

MAKES: 4 filled crepes
PREP TIME: 5 minutes, plus 2 hours to freeze
COOK TIME: 5 minutes
TOTAL TIME: 2 hours 10 minutes

VE **GF** Recommended Crepe(s): Any sweet batter | Recommended Fold(s): Triangle

My candy bar of choice is a peanut butter cup, and I like it even better when it's frozen. So my staff and I decided to freeze our version of the candy, wrapped inside a crepe, and it turned out to be astoundingly good. The chocolate and peanut butter melt inside the warm crepe and blend into a delicious mix, and when frozen, it becomes a brand-new treat.

Batter for 4 crepes
½ cup smooth peanut butter
½ cup chocolate chips

1. Prepare the crepes according to the batter instructions.

2. While the crepes are still warm, spread peanut butter over half of each crepe. You may want to pipe the peanut butter with a pastry bag to avoid tearing the crepe.

3. Sprinkle with chocolate chips and fold the crepe in half, then in half or thirds again. Let the crepe sit until the chocolate and peanut butter start to melt.

4. Once the crepe has started to cool, wrap it in foil or plastic wrap and place it in the freezer. Repeat with the remaining crepes

and freeze for at least 2 hours.

5. When you are ready to serve a crepe, carefully unwrap the covering and place it on a plate or eat it with your hands like a candy bar.

Per serving: Calories: 474; Total fat: 38g; Carbohydrates: 22g; Fiber: 4g; Protein: 15g

Ice Cream Crepe Cones

MAKES: 4 filled crepes
PREP TIME: 5 minutes
COOK TIME: 10 minutes
TOTAL TIME: 15 minutes

VE **GF** Recommended Crepe(s): Any sweet batter | Recommended Fold(s): Cone

I've always loved a good waffle cone with ice cream, but after I tried this crepe technique, it became my cone of choice. The crepe cone is seen more often in Japan, but you will certainly impress your friends when you present dessert in this delicious cone. You can use any batter, but I would suggest using the sweet version to pair with the ice cream. You can substitute any type of sauce or ice cream to suit your dietary needs.

Batter for 4 crepes
Ice cream of your choice
Chocolate or butterscotch sauce

1. Prepare the crepes according to the batter instructions, making sure they are golden brown and crisp before flipping. If the crepes are not properly cooked, they will be too flimsy to hold the ice cream.

2. Remove each finished crepe from the pan and place it on a plate.

3. Fold the crepe in half and then place a scoop of ice cream on the upper-right third of the crepe. Fold the left edge up to cover

the ice cream. Continue to roll, keeping the edges of the crepe at the top to form a cone shape.

4. Serve on a plate and garnish with drizzle of chocolate or butterscotch sauce.

Troubleshooting Tip: *To prevent the crepes from drying out, it's best to make one crepe at a time and then fill and serve it, rather than cook all the crepes at once and stack them.*

Per serving: Calories: 392; Total fat: 21g; Carbohydrates: 43g; Fiber: 2g; Protein: 9g

Bananas Foster Crepe Cake

MAKES: 8 slices crepe cake
PREP TIME: 15 minutes, plus 2 hours to chill
COOK TIME: 1 hour
TOTAL TIME: 3 hours 15 minutes

VE **GF** **Recommended Crepe(s): Any sweet batter**

Need to make a statement? Look no further. This is one of the most flavorful and impressive desserts you can possibly serve. Bananas Foster makes the perfect filling that's just the right consistency to keep the cake from becoming soggy or messy. Enjoy!

Batter for 24 crepes
8 tablespoons butter
2 cups brown sugar
2 teaspoons ground cinnamon
1 tablespoon vanilla extract
Pinch salt
7 ripe bananas, sliced
½ cup dark rum

1. Prepare the crepes according to the batter instructions, then transfer them to a rack to cool. Once cooled, place the crepes on a baking sheet and cover with a towel to keep them from drying out. Repeat this process to make a total of 24 crepes.

2. Melt the butter in a large, deep saucepan over medium-low heat. Add the sugar, cinnamon, vanilla, and salt to the pan. Stir to dissolve, then add the sliced bananas.

3. When the slices begin to brown and soften, carefully add the

163

rum. Light the pan with a long match or kitchen torch. Remove from the heat and allow the flames to subside.

4. Let the mixture cool and mash the bananas until they're thick and pureed.

5. To assemble, lay a crepe on a plate and cover with banana filling, leaving a ¼-inch border all around the edge. Repeat for a total of 22 stacked crepes, layering each crepe directly above the first and ending with a crepe on top. Cover and chill for 2 hours or more before serving.

Troubleshooting Tip: *You'll make 24 crepes in step 1, even though the cake uses only 22 crepes—just in case one or two tear during the process. Feel free to snack on any crepe casualties while the cake is chilling.*

Per serving: Calories: 894; Total fat: 52g; Carbohydrates: 87g; Fiber: 6g; Protein: 19g

Measurement Conversions

VOLUME EQUIVALENTS	U.S. STANDARD	U.S. STANDARD (OUNCES)	METRIC (APPROXIMATE)
LIQUID	2 tablespoons	1 fl. oz.	30 mL
	¼ cup	2 fl. oz.	60 mL
	½ cup	4 fl. oz.	120 mL
	1 cup	8 fl. oz.	240 mL
	1½ cups	12 fl. oz.	355 mL
	2 cups or 1 pint	16 fl. oz.	475 mL
	4 cups or 1 quart	32 fl. oz.	1 L
	1 gallon	128 fl. oz.	4 L
DRY	⅛ teaspoon	—	0.5 mL
	¼ teaspoon	—	1 mL
	½ teaspoon	—	2 mL
	¾ teaspoon	—	4 mL
	1 teaspoon	—	5 mL
	1 tablespoon	—	15 mL
	¼ cup	—	59 mL
	⅓ cup	—	79 mL
	½ cup	—	118 mL
	⅔ cup	—	156 mL
	¾ cup	—	177 mL
	1 cup	—	235 mL
	2 cups or 1 pint	—	475 mL
	3 cups	—	700 mL
	4 cups or 1 quart	—	1 L
	½ gallon	—	2 L
	1 gallon	—	4 L

OVEN TEMPERATURES

FAHRENHEIT	CELSIUS (APPROXIMATE)
250°F	120°C
300°F	150°C
325°F	165°C
350°F	180°C
375°F	190°C
400°F	200°C
425°F	220°C
450°F	230°C

WEIGHT EQUIVALENTS

U.S. STANDARD	METRIC (APPROXIMATE)
½ ounce	15 g
1 ounce	30 g
2 ounces	60 g
4 ounces	115 g
8 ounces	225 g
12 ounces	340 g
16 ounces or 1 pound	455 g

Made in the USA
Las Vegas, NV
26 May 2024